The
Boxer

An Owner's Guide To

A HAPPY HEALTHY PET

Howell Book House

Howell Book House
A Simon & Schuster Macmillan Company
1633 Broadway
New York, NY 10019

Library of Congress Cataloging-in-Publication Data
Abraham, Stephanie.
　　　　The boxer: an owner's guide to a happy, healthy pet/Stephanie
　　　　Abraham
　　　　p. cm.
　　　　ISBN: 0-87605-394-0
　　　　1. Boxers (Dogs). I. Title.
SF429.B75A37 1996
636.7'3—dc20　　　　95-41271
　　　　CIP

Manufactured in the United States of America
10　9　8　7　6　5

Series Director: Dominique De Vito
Series Assistant Director: Ariel Cannon
Book Design: Michele Laseau
Cover Design: Iris Jeromnimon
Illustration: Jeff Yesh
Photography:
　Cover Photos by Stephanie Abraham and Judy Strom
　Courtesy of the American Kennel Club: 16
　Courtesy of Ken-L Ration: 93
　Courtesy of Stephanie Abraham: 5, 8, 18, 23, 24, 29, 51
　Marcia Adams: 7, 10, 31, 33, 34, 36, 42, 44, 46, 49, 54, 65, 70, 93
　Joan Balzarini: 96
　Mary Bloom: 82, 96, 136, 145
　Paulette Braun/Pets by Paulette: 2, 9, 64
　Buckinghamhill American Cocker Spaniels: 148
　Sian Cox: 134
　Dr. Ian Dunbar: 98, 101, 103, 111, 116–117, 122, 123, 127
　Dan Lyons: 96
　Scott McKiernan: 11, 35, 50, 57, 67, 68, 69, 83
　Cathy Merrithew: 129
　Liz Palika: 133
　Janice Raines: 132
　Judith Strom: title page, 39, 47, 58, 66, 84, 96, 107, 110, 128, 130, 135,
　　　137 ,139, 140, 144, 149, 150
　Kerrin Winter & Dale Churchill: 96–97
Production Team: Trudy Brown, Jama Carter, Kathleen Caulfield, Trudy Coler,
　Amy DeAngelis, Pete Fornatale, Matt Hannafin, Kathy Iwasaki, Vic Peterson,
　Terri Sheehan, Marvin Van Tiem, and Kathleen Varanese

Contents

Welcome
to the
World
of the

part one

Boxer

External Features of the Boxer

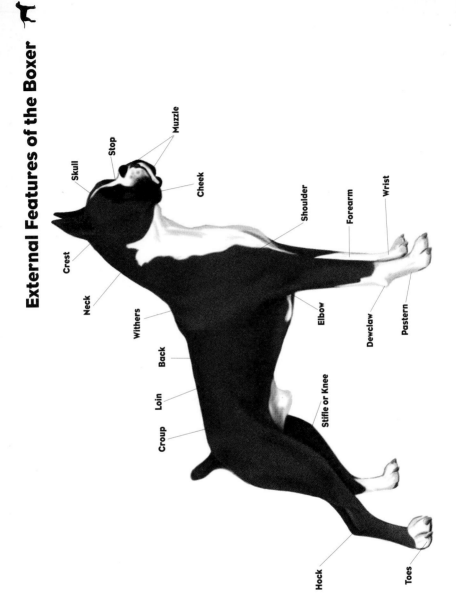

chapter 1

What
Is a
Boxer?

Congratulations! You have decided to share your life with a Boxer, one of the most engaging breeds in dogdom. I hope that the following chapters will help you to understand your Boxer, and to care for him so that he lives a long and happy life.

He will return all the love and affection you give— and then some. He will protect you; he will make you laugh on the darkest days; and he will outwit you when he feels the need. His loyalty will astonish you; his energy will exhaust you; and always his devotion will be constant.

The Standard for the Boxer

All purebred dogs are bred to a particular "standard," a type of blueprint of the breed (for more, see the "What Is a Breed Standard?" box, below). The most recent revision of the Official Breed Standard of the Boxer was adopted by the American Kennel Club on May 1, 1989. Important excerpts are reprinted at the end of this chapter for your review and reference.

WHAT IS A BREED STANDARD?

A breed standard—a detailed description of an individual breed—is meant to portray the *ideal* specimen of that breed. This includes ideal structure, temperament, gait, type—all aspects of the dog. Because the standard describes an ideal specimen, it isn't based on any particular dog. It is a concept against which judges compare actual dogs and breeders strive to produce dogs. At a dog show, the dog that wins is the one that comes closest, in the judge's opinion, to the standard for its breed. Breed standards are written by the breed parent clubs, the national organizations formed to oversee the well-being of the breed. They are voted on and approved by the members of the parent clubs.

Several parts of the written standard, however, warrant some detailed discussion and explanation. Descriptions in quotation marks are from the official standard; my commentary on the particular feature follows.

Despite a current fashion to breed taller Boxers, the standard tells us that the Boxer "is a medium-sized, square built dog," and further defines "medium-sized" as: "Adult males—22 to 25 inches; females—21 to 23 inches at the withers. Preferably, males should not be under the minimum nor females over the maximum."

Boxers are not disqualified or even penalized for slight deviations from these ideals, but major departures are undesirable. A taller dog who is to remain square will, of course, have a commensurately longer body to go with his greater height. The overall impression, then, is of a noticeably bigger, heavier animal than is called for in the standard.

Head

The standard says, "The chiseled head imparts to the Boxer a unique individual stamp." The essence of breed type in the Boxer is embodied in his head—

from the bone structure to the mood-mirroring quality of his eye expression to the formation of his lips and chin. The head is what sets him apart from other breeds and is what those who know him think of as beautiful. To the uninitiated, the Boxer head may appear bizarre, but it was developed to allow him to do the job that man required of him historically. He had to be able to catch and hold game until his master caught up to him. While his jaws, by necessity, had to have great strength, he also had to be able to breathe with his mouth embedded in thick folds of hide and fur. These requirements were satisfied by his head's unique structure.

Muzzle

"The beauty of the head depends on the harmonious proportion of muzzle to skull." The muzzle should be two-thirds the width of the skull and one-third the length of the head from the occiput to the tip of the nose. The occiput is the slightly rounded bony protuberance between the ears. Skin wrinkles appear on the forehead and contribute to the Boxer's unique, slightly quizzical expression. They are desirable but should not be excessive (referred to as "wet").

Eyes

The Boxer's eyes are a dark brown color—the deeper shades preferred. They must not be yellowish ("bird of prey" eyes). Neither should they be too round or owlish, nor too small. They reflect the dog's moods to an extraordinary degree, which the new owner will soon learn to his advantage. In combination, the Boxer's eyes and wrinkles create an expression—a "look"—that is uniquely his.

The Boxer's head is a distinctive feature of the breed, as Trefoil's Meistersinger proves.

7

Ears

Adding to the characteristic appearance of the breed in the U.S. are the Boxer's ears, which are usually "cropped"—surgically trimmed and shaped to stand upright. If you don't plan to show your Boxer, ear cropping is optional, and is in fact prohibited in the U.K. and discouraged in other parts of Europe. Ears are cropped most commonly when the puppy is between six and twelve weeks old. As the Boxer was originally bred to catch and hold game—sometimes wild boar and other sizable prey—it was desirable that he not have long, flapping, easily wounded ears. What began as a purely utilitarian practice ultimately became the fashion. As the AKC standard says, the ears are "set at the highest points of the sides of the skull." An attractive crop, somewhat tapering and long, enhances the expression.

The Boxer's jaws were designed to give him "an almost unshakable grip"; today that "grip" is around the owner's heart.

Skull

The Boxer's skull is slightly arched on top, not too flat nor rounded. "The forehead shows a slight indentation between the eyes and forms a distinct stop with the topline of the muzzle." One of the most important features of the Boxer's head is that the "tip of the nose should lie slightly higher than the root of the muzzle." In other words, the nose should tip up slightly. Historically it is essential in a correct head so that the dog may breathe while holding his prey. Note that the "tip-up" is very visible in profile. Note also that the muzzle protrudes slightly in front of the nose, further ensuring the ability to breathe. The shape of the muzzle is influenced by the

"formation of both jawbones . . . through the placement of the teeth . . . and . . . through the texture of
the lips."

Jaws

The Boxer is undershot; that is,
the lower jaw protrudes beyond
the upper jaw "and curves slightly
upward," ideally with "the corner
upper incisors fitting snugly back
of the lower canine teeth," giving
the Boxer an almost unshakable
grip. "The front surface of the
muzzle is broad and squarish."
The canine teeth beneath the full
lips contribute greatly to this
look. They should be wide apart
in both upper and lower jaws.
The row of lower incisors should
be straight, while the upper
incisors should be slightly convex.

*The Boxer is
always alert to
strange noises
or occurrences.*

The distance between upper and lower jaws should be
definitive but not so pronounced as to ever show teeth
or tongue when the mouth is closed. A wry mouth—
where upper and lower jaws are slightly askew and out
of line with each other—is a very serious fault. The lips
meet evenly in front. They are padded and thick, and
the upper lip is supported by the canines of the lower
jaw beneath. The Boxer's chin must be prominent and
visible both from the front and in profile.

Body

A natural athlete, the Boxer is designed for speed and
endurance when required, reflecting his origins as a
hunter, as well as his modern roles of guard and companion dog. While an "elegant" appearance, especially
in the show ring, is attractive and often desirable, he
must never be "weedy." Never must there be anything
less than an impression of real "substance"—the
natural consequence of strong bone and superbly
conditioned muscle.

When we say that the Boxer is a "square" dog, we mean the following: a vertical line drawn from the highest point of the withers to the ground should equal a horizontal line drawn from the foremost projection of the chest (sternum) to the rear projection of the upper thigh. To achieve squareness, the Boxer cannot be long through the loin or the back. If he does exhibit these faults, he will inevitably look "long," and the square, balanced appearance that is an essential feature of the breed will be lost.

Neck

That balance is further characterized by the neck being of adequate length and exhibiting an elegant arch as it blends smoothly into the withers (the highest point of the shoulders).

Topline

The Boxer's topline—the back—is firm and straight, and slopes slightly to the croup.

Tail

The tail is set on high, "carried upward." Customarily it is docked, and anyone who has witnessed the furiously wagging tail of a happy Boxer will see the wisdom of docking. Not only would the long tail be a menace to furniture and toddlers, it would also be subject to injury and trauma. Docking is carried out when puppies are only a few days old. At the same time, front dewclaws (vestigial claws a few inches above the paw) are removed to prevent their snagging and tearing later in life.

This Boxer is a brindle with striking white markings.

Chest and Forechest

The chest and forechest are "well defined." The brisket must reach to the elbows. "The depth of the body at the lowest point of the brisket equals half the height of the dog at the withers." If this depth is not achieved, the Boxer will look slimmer and less substantial than he should. The deep chest allows ample room for heart and lungs and contributes to endurance during strenuous physical activity. The ribs are well-defined but not shaped like a barrel so as to give a rotund appearance. The lower line of the stomach is noticeably arched in "a graceful curve to the rear." This is simply referred to as "tuck up."

Hindquarters

The angulation of the bones of the hindquarters must be in balance with the angulation of the shoulder assembly. "The upper arm is long, approaching a right angle to the shoulder blade." The rear quarters are well-angulated at the stifle (the "knee").

Gait

The balance of front and rear angulation of the bones allows the Boxer to cover ground in a smooth, effortless stride, with his back level and "adequate reach to prevent interference" of the front legs with the driving rear. This essential structure of front and rear is designed to give the Boxer maxi-

This beautiful Boxer is competing at the Westminster Kennel Club show at Madison Square Garden in New York.

mum power to chase and maneuver. A stilted, ineffi cient gait results when inadequate angulation of the front and rear quarters prevents the Boxer's ideal, ground-covering reach and drive.

Colors

The Boxer's acceptable colors are fawn (shades of tan) and brindle ("clearly defined black stripes on a fawn background"). Brindling may be sparse, with only a few stripes, to exceedingly heavy, where the fawn background barely shows at all. This is known as "reverse" brindling. Both colors are equally acceptable. They are enhanced by attractive white markings, which "must not exceed ¹/₃ of the entire coat." In other words, if you could imagine the dog laid out like a bearskin rug, the white markings, including those on the stomach, must not exceed one-third of the body area.

Typically, white markings occur on the face in the form of a blaze and/or a portion of white on the muzzle. If the dog has white markings on the face, they will "replace a part of the otherwise essential black mask." The dog may also have varying amounts of white on her front and rear legs, and a white chest and throat. White should not occur on the stifle or on the back of the torso proper," nor should it be so excessive on the face as to detract from "true Boxer expression." Totally white or almost totally white Boxers are not uncommon in a litter of puppies. Members of the American Boxer Club are pledged not to register or sell these puppies. Nor should they ever be bred, as to do so will alter the essential color patterns in the breed. While they are ineligible to compete in the show ring, they can be exhibited in obedience trials.

THE AMERICAN KENNEL CLUB

Familiarly referred to as "the AKC," the American Kennel Club is a nonprofit organization devoted to the advancement of purebred dogs. The AKC maintains a registry of recognized breeds and adopts and enforces rules for dog events including shows, obedience trials, field trials, hunting tests, lure coursing, herding, earthdog trials, agility and the Canine Good Citizen program. It is a club of clubs, established in 1884 and composed, today, of over 500 autonomous dog clubs throughout the United States. Each club is represented by a delegate; the delegates make up the legislative body of the AKC, voting on rules and electing directors. The American Kennel Club maintains the Stud Book, the record of every dog ever registered with the AKC, and publishes a variety of materials on purebred dogs, including a monthly magazine, books and numerous educational pamphlets. For more information, contact the AKC at the address listed in Chapter 13, "Resources," and look for the names of their publications in Chapter 12, "Recommended Reading."

Character

The character and temperament of the Boxer make her unique among dogs. She is "instinctively a hearing guard dog." This means that she is always alert to strange noises or unusual occurrences that she might perceive as a threat to either herself or her family. A Boxer should be fearless, ready to defend and protect. Above all, however, a Boxer loves people—especially children. She is a boisterous, happy dog, always ready for a game or a romp in the woods. She responds with delight to "friendly overtures honestly rendered." No longer a hunter of boar or bear, she is happiest with the family that she will love beyond measure.

The Official Standard for the Boxer

Due to space constraints, the standard is not printed in its entirety. For a copy of the complete Official Standard for the Boxer, contact the American Kennel Club (the address is listed in Chapter 13).

General Appearance   The *ideal* Boxer is a medium-sized, square built dog of good substance with short back, strong limbs and short, tight-fitting coat. His well-developed muscles are clean, hard and appear smooth under taut skin. His movements denote energy. The gait is firm, yet elastic, the stride free and ground-covering, the carriage proud. Developed to serve as guard, working and companion dog, he combines strength and agility with elegance and style. His expression is alert and temperament steadfast and tractable.

The chiseled head imparts to the Boxer a unique individual stamp. It must be in correct proportion to the body. The broad, blunt muzzle is the distinctive feature, and great value is placed upon its being of proper form and in balance with the skull.

In judging the Boxer, first consideration is given to general appearance, to which attractive color and arresting style contribute. Next is overall balance, with special attention devoted to the head, after which the individual body components are examined for their correct construction, and efficiency of gait is evaluated.

Head   The beauty of the head depends upon harmonious proportion of muzzle to skull. The blunt muzzle is one third the length of the head from the occiput to the tip of the nose, and two thirds the width of the skull. The head should be clean, not showing deep wrinkles (wet). Wrinkles typically appear upon the forehead when ears are erect, and folds are always present from the lower edge of the stop running downward on both sides of the muzzle. *Expression*—Intelligent and alert. *Eyes*—Dark brown in color, not too small, too protruding or too deep-set. Their mood-mirroring character, combined with the wrinkling of the forehead, gives the Boxer head its unique quality of expressiveness. *Ears*—Set at the highest points of the sides of the skull, are cropped, cut rather long and tapering, raised when alert. *Skull*—The top of the skull is slightly arched, not rounded, flat or noticeably broad, with the occiput not overly pronounced. The forehead shows a slight indentation between the eyes and forms a distinct stop with the topline of the muzzle. The cheeks should be relatively flat and not bulge (cheekiness), maintaining the clean lines of the skull, and should taper into the muzzle in a slight, graceful curve.

Body   The chest is of fair width, and the forechest well defined and visible from the side. The brisket is deep, reaching down to the elbows; the depth of the body at the lowest point of the brisket equals half the height of the dog at the withers. The ribs, extending far to the rear, are well arched but not barrel shaped. The back is short, straight and muscular. The lower stomach line is slightly tucked up, blending into a graceful curve to the rear. The croup is slightly sloped, flat and broad. Tail is set high, docked and carried upward. Pelvis long and in females especially broad.

Faults—Short heavy neck. Chest too broad, too narrow or hanging between shoulders. Lack of forechest. Hanging stomach. Slab-sided rib cage. Long or narrow loin, weak union with croup. Falling off of croup. Higher in rear than in front.

Coat   Short, shiny, lying smooth and tight to the body.

Color   The colors are fawn and brindle. Fawn shades vary from light tan to mahogany. The brindle ranges from sparse but clearly defined black stripes on a fawn background to such a heavy concentration of black striping that the essential fawn background color barely, although clearly, shows through (which may create the appearance of "reverse brindling"). White marking should be of such distributions to enhance the dog's appearance, but may not exceed one-third of the entire coat. They are not desirable on the flanks or on the back of the torso proper. On the face, white may replace part of the otherwise essential black mask and may extend in an upward path between the eyes, but it must not be excessive, so as to detract from true Boxer expression. *Faults*—Unattractive or misplaced white markings. *Disqualification*—Boxers that are any color other than fawn or brindle. Boxers with a total of white marking exceeding one third of the entire coat.

Character and Temperament   These are of paramount importance in the Boxer. Instinctively a "hearing" guard dog, his bearing is alert, dignified and self-assured. In the show ring, his behavior should exhibit constrained animation. With family and friends, his temperament is fundamentally playful, yet patient and stoical with children. Deliberate and wary with strangers, he will exhibit curiosity but, most importantly, fearless courage if threatened. However, he responds promptly to friendly overtures honestly rendered. His intelligence, loyal affection and tractability to discipline make him a highly desirable companion. *Faults*—Lack of dignity and alertness. Shyness.

chapter 2

The
Boxer's
Ancestry

The world-famous Ch. Dorian von Marienhof of Mazelaine, a foundation sire of the breed.

The Boxer's origins are ancient. His ancestors can be traced back to the Assyrians (2300–600 B.C.), who used war dogs with "heavy heads, wide short muzzles, powerful build, and great courage" (*The Boxer*, by John P. Wagner, New York: Orange Judd Publishing Co., 1953). These animals were used by hunters to run down and hold game— bear, boar and bison.

In Germany, these heavy "Bullenbeissers" (bull biters) were held in great esteem, and "throughout the Middle Ages the Bullenbeisser was Germany's only hunting hound." (*Ibid*). With the advent of the Napoleonic wars, the old ducal estates disbanded; boar and bear hunting almost ceased; and a preference for a less ponderous Bullenbeisser ensued. This fashion also satisfied a growing demand for agile fighting dogs, popular in England and the Continent.

Establishing the Boxer

By selecting for type and function, breeders developed a smaller and lighter dog from the purest old Bullenbeisser bloodlines. The modern Boxer and English Bulldog are a result of this process.

In the 1830s the English exported to Germany a particular dog they called at the time a Bulldog but who was an animal rather resembling a small Mastiff. This dog appears twice in the pedigrees of early German Boxers, and with his genes came the white color and markings that had hitherto been unknown in the Bullenbeisser. He may also have been useful in fixing head type in the Boxer.

In 1896 the first Boxer club, called the Deutscher Boxer Club, was formed in Munich. Other German Boxer clubs followed. The first German breed standard was written and adopted in 1902. In 1905 all the German clubs combined and approved the Munich Standard and Stud Book.

Though the Boxer's use as a fearless hunter gradually declined, he was valued in the 19th century as a participant in the cruel sport of bullbaiting. Many a spectator lost and won large sums betting on the outcome of such contests. The Boxer would hold onto the bull's nose with fierce intent, and the bull would attempt to dislodge the dog by any means possible.

WHERE DID DOGS COME FROM?

It can be argued that dogs were right there at man's side from the beginning of time. As soon as human beings began to document their existence, the dog was among their drawings and inscriptions. Dogs were not just friends, they served a purpose: There were dogs to hunt birds, pull sleds, herd sheep, burrow after rats—even sit in laps! What your dog was originally bred to do influences the way it behaves. The American Kennel Club recognizes over 140 breeds, and there are hundreds more distinct breeds around the world. To make sense of the breeds, they are grouped according to their size or function. The AKC has seven groups:

1) Sporting, 2) Working,
3) Herding, 4) Hounds,
5) Terriers, 6) Toys,
7) Nonsporting

Can you name a breed from each group? Here's some help: (1) Golden Retriever; (2) Doberman Pinscher; (3) Collie; (4) Beagle; (5) Scottish Terrier; (6) Maltese; and (7) Dalmatian. All modern domestic dogs (*Canis familiaris*) are related, however different they look, and are all descended from *Canis lupus*, the gray wolf.

Terrible injuries to both dog and bull resulted, and the "sport" was eventually banned. Many lithographs, notably the work of Henry Alken in England, depict these encounters; the dogs who were used bear a definite resemblance to today's Boxer, although they had long tails and were not so tall.

The development and refinement of the breed—until the 1940s, when the U.S. became involved in a meaningful way—must be credited to the Germans. The early German breeders exhibited their dogs in shows after the formation of their Boxer Clubs, and a detailed record of their pedigrees exists so that we can see the clear ancestry of the modern Boxer from about 1890. In Germany many breeders contributed to the breed in those early days of record-keeping, but in America no one has had so great an influence as the famous von Dom kennels of Philip and Friederun Stockmann.

The von Dom Boxers

The first von Dom Boxer was registered in Germany in 1911. From modest beginnings, and with considerable travail, Frau Stockmann bred some of the finest Boxers the world had yet seen. Her devotion to her dogs was legendary, and she worked tirelessly to keep them fed and warm in an increasingly politically unstable Germany.

Am./Can. Ch. Gray Roy's Minstrel Boy, one of the breed's top sires and show dogs.

Both Philip Stockmann and several of the von Dom standards were sent to the front lines when WWI broke out. The Munich Boxer Club initially sent sixty Boxers to the war effort. These dogs were used both to guard prisoners and as sentries. In addition, they would sometimes be sent out to catch and bring down an enemy soldier—actions harking back to their earlier hunting exploits in the forest.

The first von Dom connection to the U.S. was made in 1914 when Philip Stockmann returned from a show in Hamburg and announced to his wife that he had sold his dog Dampf von Dom after he had been awarded the "Sieger" (championship) title. At only eighteen months of age, Dampf was imported to America, to the then-governor of New York, Herbert H. Lehman.

Unfortunately, because so few Boxer bitches existed in this country at the time, Dampf was not often used as a stud dog. He was a son of the Stockmann's great brindle Champion Rolf v. Vogelsberg. Rolf was recognized on a Munich street as a superlative specimen and was immediately purchased by a doctor who, in turn, sold him to the Stockmanns. Although Rolf left for war duty at the age of six and did not return until he was eleven, he left behind progeny that became the foundation of the von Dom strain.

International champion Sigurd von Dom shown with Mrs. Miriam Breed.

Although the first Boxer to be registered in the U.S. was reorded by the AKC in 1904, Dampf became the first American Boxer champion in 1915.

The Cornerstones of the American Boxer

It is generally agreed that the modern Boxer in America owes his existence to four great foundation sires, all imported from Germany in the 1930s. They are the following:

- Sigurd von Dom of Barmere, a fawn dog imported by Charles Ludwig for Mrs. Miriam Breed in 1934. (Sigurd was the grandfather of the next three.)
- Dorian von Marienhof of Mazelaine, a brindle dog imported in 1935 by John and Mazie Wagner.

- Lustig von Dom of Tulgey Wood, a fawn dog imported in 1937 by Erwin Freund.

- Utz von Dom of Mazelaine, a fawn dog imported by John and Mazie Wagner in 1939. (Utz and Lustig were full brothers.)

Pioneers in the Breed

There was a small but dedicated contingent of Boxer enthusiasts in America in the early years of this century. The American Boxer Club itself, the breed's parent club in this country, was founded in 1935. These pioneering enthusiasts included G. J. Jeuther, who finished the championship of the second Boxer to attain a championship title in the U.S.: Ch. Bluecher v. Rosengarten. In 1931, Dr. Benjamin Birk imported German dogs as foundation stock for his Birkbaum kennels; in 1932, Marcia and Joseph Fennessey's Check v. Hennenstein finished as the third U.S. Boxer champion; and in 1933, Henry Stoecker of New Jersey finished Dodi v.d. Stoeckersburg, a brindle bitch who was the first female champion in the U.S. and the first to be whelped (born) in America, though she was German bred as her dam had come to this country in whelp.

In 1934, Mr. Stoecker finished Lord v.d. Stoeckersburg, who was the first American-bred champion and a half brother to Dodi out of the same dam. In 1936, the AKC moved Boxers from the Non-Sporting to the Working Group. This occasioned considerable dismay among many fanciers who felt that the Boxer could not compete successfully against the popular Doberman or Collie. In time, however, their fears were to prove unfounded.

In 1938, Philip Stockman of Germany was invited to judge the ABC Specialty. He awarded Best of Breed to the legendary Lustig. Herr Stockmann attended the ABC annual meeting that week, and his advice was sought in regard to the breed standard. One of his suggestions was that Boxers who were over one-third white be disqualified. Although at least one "Check" had by that time finished his U.S. championship, the ABC adopted the disqualification provision. It stands today.

The Mazelaine Kennels

From 1934 to 1964, John and Mazie Wagner of Wisconsin bred or owned 123 champions under the banner of their Mazelaine Kennels. They were responsible for the importation of two of the great foundation sires of the breed: Dorian (sire of forty champions) and Utz (sire of thirty-seven champions).

The Wagners were blessed with a rare combination of talents: a real appreciation of breed type and a scientific understanding of the best ways to produce it. The genetic prepotence their dogs left behind was of singular importance in the breed, and it can be said that most modern Boxers today probably trace back to one or more animals Mazelaine owned or bred.

The Barmere Kennels

It was Mrs. William Z. Breed of Barmere Kennels in New York and later California who commissioned Charles Ludwig to bring Sigurd back to her from Germany. Sigurd went on to sire twenty-six champions in the U.S. and the famous Barmere Kennels were responsible for finishing the titles of more than fifty Boxers. Mrs. Breed also imported the sire of the brothers Lustig and Utz, Zorn v. Dom, who gave us eleven champions in his own right. Dodi v.d. Stoeckersburg, aforementioned as the first bitch champion in the U.S., was purchased by Mrs. Breed to become her foundation bitch in 1933. The last champion to carry the Barmere name finished in 1963.

The Great Lustig

The great Lustig von Dom sired forty-one champions for Mr. Erwin Freund's Tulgey Wood Kennels of Illinois. If Mrs. Stockmann of Germany had not needed the money to support the rest of her v. Dom Boxers, she would never have parted with her dear Lustig. He came to the U.S. wearing a collar with the inscription

**FAMOUS
OWNERS OF
THE BOXER**

Elvis Presley

Shirley Temple

Humphrey
Bogart

Lauren Bacall

Nat King Cole

Joan Crawford

Sylvester
Stallone

Ice-T

"I am the magnificent Lustig." Years later, Mrs. Stockmann visited his grave at Tulgey Wood.

Mr. Freund finished twenty-seven champions from 1937 to 1947. At his death the kennel was taken over by his manager, Bob Rogers, who in turn died in 1950. Mazie Wagner eventually purchased the magnificent Tulgey Wood estate and designed a Boxer cemetery there. Next to Lustig are buried Dorian, Utz, and Ch. Mazelaine's Zazarac Brandy (nineteen champions). It is a touching memorial.

More Early Breeders

Other notable breeders from the early years of Boxers in America include Dr. Lewis Daniels, who owned Mazelaine's Kapellmeister, sire of thirty-three champions in the 1950s; Mrs. Ida Gaertner and her daughter, Mrs. Harold Palmedo and their Sumbula kennels; Mr. Valentine Martin and his Stuttgarter Kennels; Henry Lark; Francis Bilger; Charles Ludwig; Fred Hamm; Dr. Walter Kearns; Dr. S. Potter Bartley; Charles O. Spannaus; Max Ketzel; and Walter Lippert.

The Middle Years

On February 17, 1949, a flashy fawn puppy bred and owned by Mr. and Mrs. R.C. Harris was whelped at their Sirrah Crest Kennels in California. He grew up to be the incomparable Ch. Bang Away of Sirrah Crest, winner of 121 all-breed Best in Shows and sire of eighty-one U.S. champions.

All About Bang Away

No other Boxer whelped before or since has come close to approximating his stunning record as a show dog or a producer. Almost every living Boxer descends from Bang Away; his prepotence was ensured, as he left behind no fewer than seven American Boxer Club (ABC) designated Sires and Dams of Merit. (In order to be a Sire or Dam of Merit, a Sire must produce at least seven champions and a Dam must produce at least four).

Bang Away's showmanship was legendary, and it was evidenced very early—at only ten weeks of age he was chosen Best in Match out of ninety puppies judged by Frau Stockmann herself, visiting in California. She referred to him as "Little Lustig." Bang Away was Winners Dog and Best of Winners (meaning he was best of all the entrants except those who had already earned championship titles) from the 9–12 Puppy class at the 1950 ABC Specialty show.

Ch. Bang Away of Sirrah Crest, shown at three months of age.

In 1951, Bang Away achieved the great distinction of being Best in Show at the Westminster Kennel Club at Madison Square Garden. He was the third Boxer to go to the top at the Garden. The others were Ch. Warlord of Mazelaine (1947) and Ch. Mazelaine's Zazarac Brandy (1949). The next Boxer to win Westminster would have to wait almost twenty years: Ch. Arriba's Prima Donna (1970).

Bang Away was a flashy Boxer, meaning he had a striking amount of white on his face and feet. Until his day, Boxers in America tended to be "plainer," marked with less white. The love affair with "flash" continues into the 1990s.

Becoming Popular

The popularity of the Boxer in America surged in the 1950s. It seemed like everywhere you looked someone was walking a Boxer down the street.

Press coverage of the three Madison Square Garden wins, plus the Boxer's natural virtues of medium size and a short and tidy haircoat, contributed to his popularity. In addition, it was becoming well-publicized that while he remained an excellent guard and watchdog, he was inordinately fond of children and a friend to almost all who approached him with good intentions. He was ranked number two in all breed registrations in 1955 and 1956.

Ch. Salgray's Fashion Plate. Salgray Boxers changed the way many looked at the breed, then and now.

Of course, all this attention rarely does a breed any lasting good, and the Boxer fell victim to "backyard" breeders out to make a fast dollar. Both health and temperament suffered as a result. However, those dedicated breeders who truly loved and admired the Boxer kept patiently breeding quality animals, and the public's mercurial tastes thankfully turned to other breeds.

The 1960s to the Present

The period of the 1960s and early '70s saw breeders developing and refining the Boxer. Their work has contributed to the taller, higher-stationed animal as we know him today. Not everyone agreed with the trends, but they are facts, nonetheless.

The Salgray Kennels

The Salgray Kennels of Daniel and Phyllis Hamilburg of Massachusetts gave the Boxer new elegance and style, and they must be considered important architects in creating this "new" Boxer.

The first Salgray champion was finished in 1955—Ch. Sally of Grayarlin. Sally was purchased from Jane Kamp (now the well-known handler and judge Jane Kamp Forsyth) and her Grayarlin kennels in 1952. In 1954, the Hamilburgs purchased a bitch who was to become Ch. Slipper of Grayarlin. When they bred her to the Bang Away son Ch. Barrage of Quality Hill (sire of forty-five champions) they produced Ch. Salgray's Battle Chief. He eventually sired twenty-three champions, among them the famous "F" litter of six champions whelped in 1961 out of Ch. Marquam Hill's Flamingo (sire of seven champions).

More important than the distinction of six champions in one litter, however, was that the litter included two dogs and a bitch who would have a great influence on the breed through their offspring. They were Ch. Salgray's Fashion Plate (sire of sixty-three champions), Ch. Salgray's Flying High (twenty-seven champions) and the bitch Ch. Salgray's Flaming Ember, who in turn produced Ch. Salgray's Ambush (thirty-three champions).

Salgray Boxers and their descendants changed the way many looked at the breed then and now. They were, in general, taller, more refined, and more elegant than the breed had been in its infancy in America. The Hamilburg's daughter, Jane Guy, continues to breed the Salgray line to this day.

The Flintwood Boxers

Dr. and Mrs. Lloyd Flint of Massachusetts established their Flintwood Boxers in the mid-1950s with the purchase of two litter sisters, the soon-to-be champions Sans Souci and Morganshern of Kresthallo. They were both Bang Away granddaughters.

The Flints entered into their breeding program with a clear and scientifically thought-out plan. Both sisters were bred to Bang Away's top producing son, Ch. Barrage. Their progeny, in turn, was bred back to aunt, uncle or cousin. This relatively close (or "line") breeding established a definite Flintwood type.

Flintwood dogs were known for beautiful heads and toplines as well as overall excellence.

From 1956–65, in only seventeen breedings, twenty-six champions were born. They included four American Boxer Club Sires of Merit and two Dams of Merit, plus the foundation bitches. Ch. Arriba's Prima Donna, already mentioned as the fourth Boxer to go Best in Show at Westminster (and the only bitch), was sired by Ch. Flintwood's Live Ammo. Ch. Hi-Tech Arbitrage, winner of the Westminster Working Group in 1994, traces back to Flintwood lines through his sire, Ch. Fiero's Tally-Ho Tailo (sire of forty champions to date). Prima Donna was owned by Dr. Theodore S. Fickes and Dr. and Mrs. P. J. Pagano. Dr. Fickes's Arriba Kennels of Massachusetts has contributed many foundation bitches to other people's breeding programs—well-known names like Woods End, Huffand, New Dawn and Karjean.

THE ARRIBA BOXERS

Beginning in 1965, the Arriba Boxers were in close physical proximity to both the Flintwood and Salgray Kennels, and to these breeders Dr. Fickes credits much of his early success. However, Arriba continues to show and breed champions to this day, with three ABC Dams of Merit and two ABC Sires of Merit to its credit. The best known of these was Ch. Arriba's Knight Revue (sire of fifteen champions), who was Winners Dog and Best of Winners at the ABC Specialty show in 1970.

THE HOLLY LANE KENNELS

The Holly Lane Kennels of Dr. E. A. and Eileen McClintock of Kansas were founded in the early 1960s. Ch. Holly Lane's Windstorm is the all-time top producing bitch in breed history, with eleven champions to her credit. Still actively breeding and showing today, Holly Lane has to date given the fancy five ABC Sires of Merit (including Ch. Holly Lane's Diamond Replay) and four ABC Dams of Merit.

THE TEXAS TRECEDERS

Hollyce Stewart and her Texas Treceder Kennels were active in the 1950s and 60s. Ann Harr took over and has continued her line into the 1990s. Mrs. Stewart's Ch. Jered's Spellbinder (fifty-six champions) son, Ch. Treceder's Selection (fourteen champions), produced both Ch. Treceder's Sequel (twenty-three champions) and Ch. Treceder's Shine Boy (twenty champions).

THE CALIFORNIA MERRILANES

Eleanor Linderholm Wood and her Merrilane Boxers of California have accounted for seventy-five (and counting!) champions since 1971. Merrilane's Mad Passion is the second top-producing bitch, with ten champions. Ch. Merrilane's April Fashion, owned by Coleman Cook, sired twenty-three champions. Merrilane Boxers have been exported to many foreign countries and their influence is certainly felt abroad as well as at home. Eleanor was co-breeder, owner and handler of the 1990 ABC "Top Twenty" winner, Ch. Merrilane's Knockout.

THE JACQUET LINE

Richard Tomita and William Scolnik began their New Jersey Jacquet line when they bred the future Ch. Jacquet's Ronel Micah in 1971. Since that date Jacquet has finished the U.S. championships of over 130 Boxers and over 225 worldwide. At present there are six Jacquet ABC Sires of Merit and seven ABC Dams of Merit. Perhaps the best known of these is Ch. Happy Ours Fortune de Jacquet (sire of thirty-five champions). Others include Urko (fifteen champions), Brass Idol, Zephan and Jolie. Jacquet and Eleanor Linderhom Wood were co-breeders of Ch. Merrilane's Knockout.

THE TURO BOXERS

Texas's Sandra Roberts and Elizabeth Esacove and their Turo Kennels have been actively breeding and exhibiting since the 1970s. Their Ch. Turo's Whisper of 5T's, daughter of A Ch. Benjoman of 5T's (sire of thirty-eight champions), owned by Dr. Robert Burke (Marquam Hills Boxers), produced Ch. Marquam Hill's Traper of Turo who, with sixty-seven champions, is the second top-producing stud dog.

In addition, Turo has bred two Westminster Group winners, Ch. Turo's Cachet (owned by Leonard and Susan Magowitz) and Ch. Keibla's Tradition of Turo (owned by Mr. and Mrs. Bruce Korson, Turo and Kitty Barker). "Tiggin" is the top-winning bitch in breed history, with fifty all-breed Bests in Show and fifty Specialty wins. The numbers of important Boxer breeders in the U.S. are legion.

More Notable Names

This chapter cannot begin to cover all the kennels that contributed to the development of the Boxer; there are literally hundreds of them, many choosing to remain small home kennels.

These include names like Anchic, Bee Mike, Boxella (established in 1945 and still active), Brayshaw, Capriana, Eldic, Evergreen, Flying Apache, Marburl, MeDon, MoonValley, Pinebrook, Rococo, Scarborough, Sigro, Talisman, Trefoil, Tudosal and Von Shorer, to mention only a few.

The Boxer in Canada

Canadian influence on the Boxer is well represented on both sides of the border by Michael Millan's brindle, Ch. Millan's Fashion Hint, a Ch. Salgray's Fashion Plate son who is the third-top-producing sire in America, with sixty-six U.S. Champions.

The Scher-Khoun Kennels of Ben and Shirley DeBoer gave us Ch. Scher-Khoun's Shadrack, in turn a Fashion Hint son who sired forty-two champions. The two Shadrack sons, Ch. Scher-Khoun's Abednego and Meshack, sired twenty-three and twenty champions, respectively. Dr. and Mrs. Frank Rouse began their

Donessle Boxers with a Shadrack daughter, Donessle's Miss Fancy (four champions, one a Dam of Merit). "Missy" was twice bred to U.S. Ch. Gray Roy's Minstrel Boy (twenty-four champions), owned by David and Stephanie Abraham and their Trefoil Boxers. This union produced four champions including Ch. Trefoil's Dylan of Donessle (sire of eight champions) and Canadian Ch. Donessle's Foxfire, a top producing dam in Canada in back of all the succeeding Donessle dogs. Notable among these is Ch. Donessle's Cassino (sire of eleven champions).

A Boxer for today, Ch. Hi-Tech Arbitrage, winner of the Working Group at Westminster, 1994.

Norah and Jim McGriskin's Aracrest Kennels were extremely active in the 1970s. They left us with three ABC Sires of Merit—Ch.s Kaylib, Jered and Talisman, all eventually sold to breeders in the U.S. Other Canadian breeders of note include Jack and Cathryn Ireland (Pinepath kennels), Eve and Stan Whitmore (Haviland kennels), Eleanor Foley (Elharlen), Judy Jury (Trimanor), Shirley Bell (Bellcrest), Mr. and Mrs. Robert Verhulst, Len and Jean Reece (Gaylord) and Mr. and Mrs. Walter Pinsker (Mephisto), breeders of two Sires of Merit, Ch.s Mephisto's Vendetta (sixteen champions and sire of Traper) and Soldier of Fortune (eleven champions).

Almost every Canadian breeder, and subsequently many in the U.S., owes a debt of gratitude to the Blossomlea Kennels of Jean Grant. Active in the 1950s and 60s, Blossomlea figures prominently in the pedigrees of many Canadian dogs, including Shadrack.

Today's Dog

In the 1980s and '90s the Boxer has settled into comfortable AKC registration figures. In 1991, '92 and '93 he ranked seventeenth out of approximately 137 breeds. He continues to enjoy a quiet but devoted following, and indeed he has been owned by many famous "fans" over the years, including Elvis Presley, Humphrey Bogart, Broderick Crawford, Lauren Bacall and Shirley Temple.

Happily, peacetime has not required him to act as a war dog, either as sentry or message-taker, as was common in both World Wars. Instead, he has become a successful guide dog for the blind, a certified specialist trained to help the physically handicapped, and a well-mannered visitor bringing cheer to nursing homes.

A True Homebody

While the Boxer is an exciting show dog, he is always happiest at home with those he loves. Indeed it is his loyalty and sweet disposition that have endeared him to his legions of admirers over the years.

chapter 3

The **World**

According to the

Boxer

A Boxer is a complicated animal. More than any other dog, her moods mirror those of her master. Her sensitivity is astonishing. While she is a great clown, always ready to run and play, she can display great courage and even aggression when needed. Her eyes are almost human in their expression, and in them you can clearly read her state of mind.

A dog with these sensitivities is no windup toy; she is not an animal who can always be counted on to do what is expected. Rather, the Boxer is often the very definition of "independence." While she may mellow with advanced age, a Boxer is a physically active dog. She loves to roughhouse—she will fetch an object and cheerfully dare her owner to take it back. She will refuse to move over if you attempt to push her aside. She has a tendency to jump up, and there is considerable muscular force behind these loving greetings.

A DOG'S SENSES

Sight: With their eyes located farther apart than ours, dogs can detect movement at a greater distance than we can, but they can't see as well up close. They can also see better in less light, but can't distinguish many colors.

Sound: Dogs can hear about four times better than we can, and they can hear high-pitched sounds especially well. Their ancestors, the wolves, howled to let other wolves know where they were; our dogs do the same, but they have a wider range of vocalizations, including barks, whimpers, moans and whines.

Smell: A dog's nose is his greatest sensory organ. His sense of smell is so great he can follow a trail that's weeks old, detect odors diluted to one-millionth the concentration we'd need to notice them, even sniff out a person under water!

Taste: Dogs have fewer taste buds than we do, so they're likelier to try anything—and usually do, which is why it's especially important for their owners to monitor their food intake. Dogs are omnivores, which means they eat meat as well as vegetable matter like grasses and weeds.

Touch: Dogs are social animals and love to be petted, groomed and played with.

Boxers Play Hard

This agile leaping is no doubt a part of her genetic heritage: Her name itself evolves from the German "Boxen," or "Boxer." Though it cannot be definitely proven, the name probably derives from the Boxer's habit of playing with her front paws. She uses these paws almost like hands: to poke, to punch and, after giving birth, to cradle puppies.

One cannot underestimate a Boxer's strength. She is quite capable of knocking an adult man to his knees. It is therefore imperative to train a Boxer to curb her natural tendencies to leap and make body contact. Remember—she was bred to overpower large animals, so these instincts come quite naturally to your Boxer.

Happily, she no longer has any interest in "holding" humans with her strong jaws. She will, however, grip a play toy with unshakeable enthusiasm, and one of her great delights is to pull with her master in a cheerful tug-of-war.

Until she is trained, your Boxer will also have an instinctive desire to pull on her leash; she could easily drag you down the street. It is obvious that she must be firmly instructed in "civilized" behavior.

She is not a dog for the proverbial "little old lady"—until she knows her manners.

Boxers Get Bored

Training your Boxer can be a challenge. You will find that she is of superior canine intelligence. This intellect, combined with her independence, demands a strong trainer, one wise in the ways of such dogs. First, we must remember that a Boxer gets bored very easily. While she can be quickly taught everything from polite behavior to parlor tricks, she will not perform reliably if she sees no point to the exercise.

Boredom may be mistaken for stubbornness by the unwary trainer. Therefore, instructing a Boxer must be made "fun" for the dog; she must look forward to these sessions, not dread them. Most (not all) trainers employ edible treats and much praise to enhance these exercises. Gradually, as the dog consistently obeys, praise replaces the goodies. And in time, certain learned behaviors, such as walking in a responsive fashion on a lead, become simple second nature to the dog.

The Boxer is a physically active dog.

While I have called your attention to the Boxer's physical strength, it must be said that all her clownish and rough-and-tumble ways are usually tempered with good judgment. While she may gallop right at you, as if to mow you down, she will turn aside at the last delicious moment.

Boxers Love Kids

He is apt to be gentler and less bold with women than with men, and when a Boxer meets children, magic happens. Boxers adore children. If you walk a Boxer down a crowded street, you will invariably find that his attention is engaged by kids of all shapes and sizes. He finds them fascinating creatures, and in your household he will almost always be found at the side of the littlest people around. Your Boxer will take any amount of abuse from a child without a thought of retaliation. Indeed, he will seem to thrive on the sometimes careless games that a child may invent for his dog—the two-year-old's "Let's pour sand in his ear" or "Let's pull his tail" game, or the seven-year-old's "Let's dress Rover up in mom's clothes" antics.

Boxers seem to understand instinctively the physical limitations of kids—from tiny tots to teens. Babies are regarded with the utmost respect, and you may often find your Boxer parked soulfully next to a crib, gently contemplating the infant therein.

Boxers adore children, and make wonderful friends and guardians.

Boxers are very protective of children, and many a mother has left her toddler briefly in a Boxer's care while her back was turned, secure in the knowledge that no harm would come to the baby if the dog was nearby. Indeed, your Boxer will have a special regard for all humans he understands to be helpless or handicapped—not only kids, but also the sick and infirm.

Boxers Like to Have Fun

A Boxer has a great sense of humor. Her antics around the house are a constant source of amusement to her human guardians. A Boxer is one of the few dogs who enjoys playing all by herself. If no human is available, she may pick up a toy or a tissue from the wastebasket (beware—wastebaskets are regarded as a Boxer's private "stash!") and parade around the house, tossing her prize not-so-delicately in the air and rolling over on it on the rug. You may return from an afternoon's shopping and find said rug swept to one side on the floor, and a Boxer greeting you with an impish glint in her eyes. Or, as in the case of a friend of ours, you may find your shoes tossed down the stairwell, a gesture clearly designed to tell you you've been absent too long!

A Boxer has an instinctive desire to be clean. She will groom herself constantly in a catlike fashion, licking off offending dirt, and using her paws to wipe her face. This natural tendency is easily channelled into quick and easy housebreaking for the young puppy: no self-respecting Boxer will have any part of soiling herself or her bed. Contrary to popular myth, a Boxer does not drool any more than most dogs. In fact, the only time she will do so is if she is constantly rewarded by begging food at the table. A Boxer does, however, accumulate water in her flews when drinking, and if she happens to shake her head soon after, onlookers beware!

Boxers can be a challenge to train, as they're very intelligent and easily bored.

Boxers definitely are not natural water dogs. Most Boxers hate to immerse even their tiniest toe in extraneous water droplets. If it is raining, and it is time for your Boxer to answer a call of nature, she will look at you in amazement at the mere *suggestion* that she should venture outside.

One of our Boxer friends owned a female Boxer who, when absolutely required to relieve herself in inclement weather, would go to the door and turn delicately around. With her front paws still on the threshold, she would do her duty and rush back inside. Before we realized the Boxer's aversion to water, my husband perversely threw a stick into a small pond on our property. Our seven-month-old puppy leapt gaily after it, only to surface in abject astonishment and disgust. Though swimming came naturally to her, she never went into the pond again in all her long life.

A Boy or a Girl?

Many people, seeking a pet for the family, will ask me which sex they should purchase. Usually, they assume that the female of the species is quieter and gentler.

While the female is certainly smaller in physical size, she is not necessarily a more gentle animal than her male counterpart. I have known females who were pure hellions and males who were calm and mellow. Gender does not predetermine your Boxer's nature, and the individual disposition of any given dog will determine his or her behavior. Of course, if you elect to breed your female, you will have to deal with the complications of her heat periods and her desire to be bred at this time.

A Boxer is one of the few dogs who enjoys playing all by herself!

A Boxer is a jealous dog. He is insistent and demanding of your affection, and thus, he is jealous of every living creature who could come between him and his family members. If one Boxer tries to curl up on your lap (an interesting feat!), you will have two Boxers vying for the same space; if the family cat gets a pat on the head, the Boxer will insist on his due. He is also jealous and possessive about objects such as toys and food dishes. If a dozen rubber "squeakies" are scattered about the rug, you can count on two Boxers coveting the same latex mouse. Likewise, food dishes are zealously guarded.

Boxers Are Selective

Boxers, as a rule, are not inordinately fond of other dogs. They would really much prefer that their world not have to be shared with other canines who might at any time occupy your attention. Sometimes, this lack of sociability can take very serious turns. Boxers have been implicated in dogfights with grave consequences. Usually, two Boxers of opposite sexes will live happily together; the trouble is more likely to erupt if two males share the same household. There may be equal nastiness if two bitches decide not to get along.

Once a Boxer takes a dislike to another dog, regardless of breed, it is very difficult, if not impossible, to change his mind. Pacifism is not a breed characteristic. Sometimes, if you are lucky, your Boxers will quietly establish a "pecking order" in the household. Without obvious signs, one dog will dominate and the others will accept his or her leadership.

Years ago we lived with three adult male Boxers in the family—a sire and two sons. These dogs were inseparable; they slept in a sloppy pile together; they ate side by side; there was never a glimmer of trouble. In the course of time, the older dog died. Within two weeks the two brothers, the same two brothers who spent all their time playing in perfect harmony, would have quite literally fought to the death. No amount of psychology ever changed the situation, and they lived behind closed doors for the rest of their lives.

THE CHARACTERISTICS OF A BOXER
Sensitive
Courageous
Athletic
Easily bored
Loves children
Playful
Clean

This situation is not an unusual one. In this particular case, it seems clear that the sire exerted dominance over the sons, and they accepted it. After his death, however, the younger animals vied for superiority, and each refused to yield. While situations like this are not unique to the Boxer breed, you must remember that they are powerful animals, and they cannot be taken for granted.

Boxers Are Not Noisy

One of the Boxer's great virtues is his relative silence. If you attend a Boxer national specialty (a dog show of just Boxers), you will be struck by the lack of canine noise you hear. That is not to say that your Boxer has no voice. Rather, he has a loud, booming, almost roaring bark when he feels the need to warn. He simply uses his vocal capabilities sparingly and only after thinking the situation over. Known as a "hearing guard dog," he will generally bark when a stranger enters his yard or another dog dares to cross his boundary line. Thus, he is a very effective watchdog. If the stranger is invited in, he will most likely become your Boxer's best friend, but we try not to publicize that fact in "Burglar World"!

I have only just touched on the essence of the Boxer. They are at once fun, frustrating, lovable, obstinate, uncannily bright, and great clowns. They will make your home a happier place. When we lose them, as we inevitably must, we shall remember the morning they stole a pound of butter from the kitchen; we shall remember the tails that wagged with delight every time they saw us; we shall remember their sweetly quizzical expressions, and their unquestioning love.

No Boxer owner will ever attempt to equate "obedience" with "intelligence." A Boxer basically does what he does when he feels like doing it—but he learns like lightning. A Boxer needs to know *why* he should do something, *why* he should interrupt his leisure to pursue some silly human desire. If you give him reason enough, the Boxer just may perform for you—and do it in style. But a Boxer without a reason is a Boxer immovable.

Boxers Are Creative

Those of us who are fortunate enough to live with a Boxer(s) can cite many instances that illustrate his innate creativity. I'm thinking of a puppy named Bo who, when placed in a crate for the first time, watched with great interest while I securely fastened the latch, then calmly reached out and carefully *lifted* the latch in a reverse pattern and calmly walked free. And did it again. And again. I'm thinking of a dog named Dylan who left for a week of dog shows without his beloved green rubber frog. When he returned home at last, he *raced* through the house, up the stairs, and behind the door where he *knew* he had left Mr. Amphibian.

I'm thinking of a dog named Gus, who rode across Long Island Sound on the auto ferry with me on one bright summer afternoon. It was a pleasurable trip (Gus' first) replete with lots of Fritos and oatmeal cookies proferred by the kids who decided Gus was ineffably fascinating. When the trip ended, we found ourselves in the middle of a long line of disembarking passengers impatiently threading their way among the tightly spaced cars on the auto deck.

Boxers get along with other animals, but most prefer the company of their owners.

Suddenly, disaster loomed. The tiny spaces had grown so small that no seventy-five-pound male Boxer could physically maneuver another step. Harried passengers glared at us without pity. We could not proceed; we could not retreat. The line halted. Without any forethought, I nervously looked down at Gus, who was anxiously looking up at me, and said something very close to the following, aloud: "Gus, there is no way we can do this, unless you get down on your belly and crawl underneath these cars so we can get out of here."

My big, sweet, full-of-cookies dog gazed right into my eyes, lowered his body, and crawled under three cars while I struggled to keep up with his end of the leash.

The fat man in front of me gasped at this prodigious intellectual feat; the pink-hatted lady behind me shook her head in disbelief; I myself was mightily impressed. Gus was justifiably proud of himself and jauntily completed his navigation of the auto maze without further complication. Obedience at short notice was his specialty.

MORE INFORMATION ON BOXERS

NATIONAL BREED CLUB

American Boxer Club
Mrs. Barbara E. Wagner, Corresponding Secretary
6310 Edward Dr.
Clinton, MD 20735-4135

The club can give you information on all aspects of the breed, including the names and addresses of smaller clubs in your area. Inquire about membership.

BOOKS

Kraupa-Tuskany, Herta F. *Boxers: A Complete Pet Owner's Manual* (Hauppage, N.Y.: Barron's Educational Series, 1988).

McFadden, Billie. *The New Boxer* (New York: Howell Book House, 1989).

Nicholas, Anna Katherine. *The Boxer* (Neptune, N.J.: TFH, 1984).

Pisano, Beverly, *Boxers.* (Neptune, N.J.: TFH, 1992).

MAGAZINES

The Boxer Quarterly
811 Spring Street
Box 125
Paso Robles, CA 93446

The Boxer Review
Drucker Publications
8760 Appian Way
Los Angeles, CA 90046

VIDEOS

American Kennel Club, *Boxers.*

Living

with a

part two

Boxer

chapter 4

Bringing Your
Boxer
Home

A Boxer puppy will bring you untold joy—and he will try your patience. He will interrupt your sleep and wreak havoc with your daily routine. He will walk through his water bowl and spit up on the rug. But he will also snuggle up beside you, lick your face, and tell you in all his extensive Boxer vocabulary that you are the greatest human on earth. He will help make life worth living.

Choosing a puppy is usually a happy expedition to a breeder's home or kennel. Do not be put off if your puppy's owner puts you through the "third degree," asking questions like, Where will the puppy sleep? Where will the puppy stay while you're at work? Do you have a fenced-in yard? If you owned a dog before, what happened to him? All of these questions are designed to determine whether yours is a suitable home for the sweet puppy the breeder has lovingly raised for his first weeks of life.

Picking Your Puppy

We shall assume you pass the "test" easily. Now, which puppy in the litter will be yours? The breeder may offer you a choice of only one or two. That's perfectly all right. There are very likely to be "reservations" for one or more of the babies—people who left deposits even before birth. Excellent breeders are sometimes booked well in advance of whelping.

If you do have a choice, be sure to pick a lively, alert animal, one who bounces up to greet you and wants to interact with the family. Do not be taken by the shy, shivering pup in the corner, no matter how "sorry" you may feel for him. Remember—he was raised under the same conditions as his littermates and for reasons unknown to you has not developed into a happy, well-adjusted animal. This could be temporary, due to a curable illness, or it could be genetic, meaning that he may grow to be an unhappy adult.

Knowing all these things well in advance of our first puppy purchase, my husband and I went one afternoon to see a litter of tumbling, bumbling eight-week-old Boxers. We had a choice of six.

Wisely, remembering the latest "dog" book he had read, my husband dropped a ring of keys into the midst of the babies. Five puppies rushed to investigate—a very good temperament test. They were curious, and not in the least shy. One pretty male pup eyed the keys, looked at us, and calmly picked up a piece of a blanket and walked under a chair to chew it. He ignored us in the extreme. Of course, we said "We'll have that one!" He grew up to be American/Canadian Champion Gray Roy's Minstrel Boy (AKA "Casey") and was an adored and well-adjusted family member for all his days.

PUPPY ESSENTIALS

Your new puppy will need:

food bowl

water bowl

collar

leash

I.D. tag

bed

crate

toys

grooming supplies

Puppy Preparations

Plans for the new arrival must be put into effect before she ever crosses your threshold. Imagine if you had a new human baby; your nursery would be ready when she came home from the hospital. So too, your puppy's new home must be made ready for her.

Take your puppy into your fenced yard or out for a walk to relieve himself.

THE CRATE

Though not actually essential, I would strongly urge you to purchase a dog crate. They come in moulded plastic or wire mesh, and you should choose a size large enough for an adult Boxer to lie in comfortably and turn around.

These crates are in the range of twenty-one inches wide and thirty-six inches long. If you buy a wire crate, be sure the mesh is not so wide your puppy can get her head through—puppies can insert their heads into very small spaces. The danger here is that they will not be able to extract themselves and may panic and choke. Having issued that warning, let me tell you that a crate will make your life much easier. They are useful for two things: housebreaking and your pup's physical safety.

As we mentioned in chapter 3, a Boxer is a naturally clean dog. She most definitely does not want to soil either herself or her bed. Therefore, if a puppy is secure in a closed crate while you are unavoidably away from home, she will try very hard to contain herself until she is set free. Believe me, it works.

A crate is also a safe haven from the bustle of family life. Remember, a new pup, like a new baby, needs a great deal of sleep. Children especially, with the best of intentions, tend not to think along those lines.

Therefore, if you keep the crate door open, you will eventually see your pup asleep on her blanket inside—a safe retreat until she is rested and ready to play once more.

Collars and Leashes

A collar and leash are important items to have on hand for the new arrival. Be sure that the collar is a flat type made of soft leather or synthetic materials. There is no need for a "choke" collar at this time.

Be sure that the flat collar is adjustable as the puppy grows, and that you fasten it so that he cannot pull it over his head. Personally, I never have a collar on either a puppy or an adult dog unless I am physically present and planning to take the dog out for a walk.

Remember that your Boxer is a physically active dog. Collars can get snagged on all manner of things: tree limbs, cabinet doors, furniture. No collar is absolutely safe. Therefore, take no chances. However, a collar and leash are very necessary to teach your puppy to walk calmly at your side.

Unless you have a fenced yard (which I urge you to create), you will need to walk your puppy while he relieves himself. Remember—a puppy can run much faster than you can, so do *not* ever let your puppy loose in a situation where he could find himself on a road. Even the quietest roads have cars occasionally, and it takes only one car to play a part in a tragic scenario.

Make sure your puppy will have all she needs before you bring her home.

The leash itself does not need to be more than six feet long and should be strong, with a quality "catch" made of sturdy metal. If you want a longer lead, the retractable "Flexi" leads are excellent. As the puppy grows older, their longer length will afford him some real exercise opportunity.

Bowls for Food and Water

Your puppy should have separate bowls for food and water. Water should be available at all times, though you may want to limit it at night. Bowls come in all shapes and sizes. The best are made of tough, weighted plastic or weighted stainless steel; the weighted feature is helpful so that the puppy cannot easily spill the bowl and contents. Be sure that bowls are not constructed of flimsy, easily splintered plastic.

HOUSEHOLD DANGERS

Curious puppies and inquisitive dogs get into trouble not because they are bad, but simply because they want to investigate the world around them. It's our job to protect our dogs from harmful substances, like the following:

IN THE HOUSE

cleaners, especially pine oil

perfumes, colognes, aftershaves

medications, vitamins

office and craft supplies

electric cords

chicken or turkey bones

chocolate

some house and garden plants, like ivy, oleander and poinsettia

IN THE GARAGE

antifreeze

garden supplies, like snail and slug bait, pesticides, fertilizers, mouse and rat poisons

Toys

Toys are important for puppies and adult dogs alike. Your Boxer revels in play, and toys are an important part of his world. If you do not supply them, your Boxer will create his own toys—by raiding the trash bin, taking a magazine off a counter, or finding your socks under the bed.

The most important toy you can give your new puppy, and one he will never tire of as long as he lives, is a sturdy, synthetic, almost indestructible bone. These are usually made of tough, hard nylon. They come in various shapes and sizes. The packaging will inform you that they are impregnated with an attractive (to dogs!) odor, but your Boxer will chew on it long after any artificial odor has wafted away.

While your puppy is teething, especially between four and six months of age, a bone is almost a necessity—it will save the furniture.

Although a Boxer is not a notorious "chewer" by nature and usually grows out of the teething stage rather quickly, why take chances with Aunt Martha's antiques? Be sure *not* to buy rawhide in any form. Boxers do love it but tend to end up with masses of it impacted in their intestines, with dire medical consequences. Natural bone can splinter and cause internal damage. Likewise, we stay away from the popular "chew hooves" and pig's feet.

Latex toys are lots of fun, especially those that contain "squeakers." Eventually, your Boxer will extract and swallow the squeaker, so beware. He will also cheerfully dismantle the latex while you watch. We only allow latex for a short play period while we are in attendance.

Soft frisbees that cannot splinter or, indeed, soft toys of any kind, are also great playthings—just watch for signs of destruction prior to consumption!

Balls are also of great appeal. Do be sure that they are soft so that they cannot break your puppy's teeth, and be certain that they are sufficiently large enough that they cannot be swallowed in one great gulp. Tennis balls are *too small*!

Your puppy will need chew toys, like the rope toy here, and a soft, comfy bed.

A Comfy Bed

Your Boxer will love a nice, soft bed. Whether she is a puppy or an adult, she likes her creature comforts. A synthetic fleece blanket in her crate, or a soft commercial dog bed available from pet supply stores, will make her very happy.

Of course, she is happiest of all in *your* bed. Allowing her the luxury of your linen is up to you—but do remember that the adorable ten-pound puppy is going to grow up to weigh many times that!

Be sure that your Boxer sleeps out of drafts; she does not have a heavy coat to keep her warm. This is especially important for the new puppy, who has, up to now, had the physical presence of her mother and littermates to keep her from the cold. A hot water bottle wrapped up in a blanket will help her to feel secure for her first days in her new home.

Puppy-Proofing

A house is a potentially dangerous place for a puppy. Remember how you put special "child-proof" locks

on doors while your toddler was growing up? A puppy requires the same assessment of her environment.

Electrical outlets, for one thing, are potential hazards. Puppies left to their own devices love to chew on outlets and cords.

Houseplants may look lovely on the windowsill, but are they lethal if swallowed? I well remember a Christmas season and a bouncy litter of twelve-week-olds. While my back was turned "only for a minute," they managed to tumble a Jerusalem cherry plant from the kitchen counter. All ended well, but my vet's cheerful admonition to administer ipecac to effect meant a very long and messy night!

Boxers don't need as much exercise as some breeds, but they enjoy a good romp.

It is wise to own a common "poison" chart and post it in an accessible location. Make sure you have the phone numbers for the National Animal Poison Control Center posted by your veterinarian's number. The NAPCC is listed in Chapter 13.

Exercise

A Boxer does not need as much exercise as you may imagine. Of course, she does love to run—but she does not need to be in an area the size of a national park to keep trim and happy.

Your first consideration must be her safety while she is loose. That is one reason why an enclosed backyard is such a great place—she can play safely there for hours.

A Boxer also does surprisingly well as an apartment dweller in the city—as long as she goes on two or three brisk walks a day and has a lot of companionship so that she does not become utterly bored with her life.

You will find that puppies, like children, play hard and then sleep deeply. This is perfectly normal. Do not let the children constantly rouse the puppy from her naps.

Cropped ears need to be taped up; be patient while they set.

Good Habits

It is wise to accustom your puppy to a routine: meals at certain times of the day, walks immediately thereafter, retiring for the night at a given hour. This schedule will foster good and lasting habits.

Everyone in the family should be aware of and help out in keeping to your puppy's schedule. The better everyone is at sticking to the schedule, the sooner your puppy will be housebroken and the calmer he'll be because he'll know what to expect from you and when.

Plan out a schedule that works for everyone in the family, but most importantly for the puppy. Whoever gets up first should let puppy out to relieve himself.

Soon thereafter, the puppy should get his morning meal, then it's right back outside to go to the bathroom again. (See Chapter 8 for guidance on housetraining.)

Someone should play with the puppy for a while, then put the pup in his crate for a nap. Later in the morning, puppy will need to go out again, eat, go out again, play, nap, go out again, perhaps nap or evening meal, out again and so on. You and your family can determine what times will be mealtimes, then schedule going outside, play and naps around them.

Identification

Your dog should always wear a collar with a tag stating your name, address and phone number. A permanent form of identification may soon be required by the American Kennel Club for all puppies.

Tattooing at an early age inside the flank or inside the ear is a common form of identification today. The implantation of a tiny coded microchip is also becoming more and more common. These identifying devices are designed to help locate your dog if he becomes lost. They are also a means to prevent unscrupulous breeders from falsifying records. You should consult your dog or pup's breeder for further information, or write to the AKC itself at 51 Madison Ave., New York, N.Y. 10010.

Cropping and Docking

When you purchase your Boxer, his tail will have undoubtedly been docked. This operation is performed within a few days of birth.

Ear cropping is commonly done between seven and twelve weeks of age. If you do plan to have the ears cropped, I recommend puchasing the puppy with this surgery behind him. The breeder is then responsible for making sure that the ears heal properly, a process that takes about two weeks. After healing, the ears are then taped upright until they stand properly. This process can take many weeks—sometimes a year.

The breeder should help you and instruct you in the proper methods of taping ears. It is *not*, unfortunately, a task that affords instant gratification. *Be patient*; the most common reason for ear failures is that the owners gave up too soon.

If the cropping is your responsibility, consult knowledgeable breeders so that you choose a veterinarian who is skilled in the procedure. Not only must he or she know how to do the surgery, but you must make certain that he or she uses appropriate anaesthesia for a young puppy.

Giving Love = Getting Love

As your Boxer grows, you will quickly learn his needs. All of the advice in this chapter will become second nature to you. Raising a puppy is much like raising a child. Your puppy needs lots of love and discipline, and an intelligent, caring provider. He will reward you with a lifetime of affection.

chapter 5

Feeding

Your

Boxer

The old adage "You are what you eat" applies to dogs as well as people. Your Boxer's daily diet is reflected in the condition of his coat, the spring in his step, and his overall outlook on life. One of the biggest favors you can do for your dog is to put the proper type and amount of food in his bowl.

About Nutrition

There are six staples of nutrition that dogs need every day: protein, carbohydrates, fats, vitamins, minerals and water. Following is a synopsis of what these provide your dog and why they're necessary. Remember, nutrition is a science, and this is the briefest of discussions. Commercial dog food manufacturers spend millions of dollars to see that their products contain the proper amounts of each nutrient category (except water, which you must provide for your dog). There are many books that go into the subject in more detail; some are listed in Chapter 12, "Recommended Reading."

Protein is used for bone growth, tissue repair and the daily replacement of body tissues used by a normally active dog. Sources of protein include meat and eggs. Protein is not stored in your dog's body, so it must be replaced every day.

Carbohydrates provide energy, help assimilate fats, and aid digestion and elimination. Sources of carbohydrates include grains such as wheat, rice, soy and corn. Carbohydrates break down into starches and sugars to provide the body with energy-efficient fuel. Excess carbohydrates are stored in the body for future use.

Fats are another necessary energy source. They also provide shine and suppleness to your dog's coat and skin. But as we all know too well, excess fat is not good for us or for our dogs, leading to obesity and its health-related problems. Getting too little fat is equally harmful, however, so maintaining a balance is important.

Vitamins contribute to numerous cellular and hormonal functions, including digestion, reproduction and growth. Vitamins are necessary for releasing nutrients from food. They are not synthesized within the body, and must be acquired from foods or supplements. Let's look at some of the vitamins that are necessary for the health of your Boxer. (Please consult your veterinarian if you want to supplement your dog's food with any vitamins.)

HOW MANY MEALS A DAY?

Individual dogs vary in how much they should eat to maintain a desired body weight—not too fat, but not too thin. Puppies need several meals a day, while older dogs may need only one. Determine how much food keeps your adult dog looking and feeling her best. Then decide how many meals you want to feed with that amount. Like us, most dogs love to eat, and offering two meals a day is more enjoyable for them. If you're worried about overfeeding, make sure you measure correctly and abstain from adding tidbits to the meals.

Whether you feed one or two meals, only leave your dog's food out for the amount of time it takes her to eat it—10 minutes, for example. Freefeeding (when food is available any time) and leisurely meals encourage picky eating. Don't worry if your dog doesn't finish all her dinner in the allotted time. She'll learn she should.

Vitamin A is necessary for a healthy, shiny coat because it is used by your dog's body for fat absorption. It is also essential for normal growth rate, reproduction and good eyesight.

The *B vitamins* protect the nervous system, and are also important for healthy skin, appetite, eyes and growth.

Vitamin C has been called a wonder vitamin for its immune-boosting and other healing properties. Studies are constantly being conducted on the properties of vitamin C, and some dog owners add it to their dog's food for the same reasons they take it themselves.

TO SUPPLEMENT OR NOT TO SUPPLEMENT?

If you're feeding your dog a diet that's correct for her developmental stage and she's alert, healthy-looking and neither over- nor underweight, you don't need to add supplements. These include table scraps as well as vitamins and minerals. In fact, a growing puppy is in danger of developing musculoskeletal disorders by over-supplementation. If you have any concerns about the nutritional quality of the food you're feeding, discuss them with your veterinarian.

Vitamin D, "the sunshine vitamin," is essential for healthy bones, teeth and muscles, but must work in conjunction with the minerals calcium and phosphorus.

Vitamin E contributes to the proper functioning of the internal and reproductive organs as well as muscles.

Minerals are in the tissues of all living things, contributing to bones, muscles, cells, nerves and blood. Like vitamins, minerals work together and individually. Minerals include *calcium* and *phosphorus, cobalt, copper, chlorine, iodine, iron, magnesium, manganese, sodium* and *zinc.*

Water is perhaps the most important nutrient of all, for without it cellular functions would cease and life would end. (More on this later in this chapter.)

Three to Six Months Old

When you bring your new puppy home from his breeder's kennel, you will undoubtedly have been supplied with a written summary of his diet to date. Whatever else you may do, *do not change* the puppy's regimen, at least not until he is well-established in your household. Baby puppies have sensitive digestive tracts, and a sudden change in food may cause them either to stop eating or develop diarrhea—both unpleasant consequences.

Most veterinarian-approved books on puppy care will advise you to feed an eight-week-old pup up to four times a day. I find that three times daily at that age is sufficient, and by the time my puppies are twelve weeks old I have them accustomed to a twice-daily schedule. They appear to thrive, and in fact they remain on this regimen for the rest of their lives. Scheduling is very important. Your puppy should become accustomed to a routine that is comfortable for his household. If you constantly change the time and place of his feedings, you will encourage a fussy and frustrated eater.

Make sure your Boxer gets fresh water whenever he wants it.

No Treats for Meals

Likewise, when you have settled on a food that your puppy likes—as well as a food that is optimally nutritious—do not allow yourself to be manipulated by your dog into substituting special treats for his regular meals. My husband grew up with a mixed breed who trained her family to feed her nothing but canned food and gizzards—hardly an ideal diet! Food should be left down for about thirty minutes and then removed until the next regular feeding. Don't worry—the chances of your finicky eater starving himself to death are minimal. Be strong!

Water! Water!

Supplying your puppy or adult dog with fresh water is one of the most important things you can do to ensure his long-term health. Our own and our canine's bodies are made up of over 66 percent water. Therefore, we need to renew this simple compound continually. While a human is supposedly intelligent enough to consume water in a variety of ways—in coffee, fruit drinks, and sodas—your dog depends on his water bowl. It should be available to him almost twenty-four hours a day. Insufficient water intake leads to a variety of serious medical conditions. One of the most common is kidney failure in the adult. In puppies, dehydration is a more immediate danger. Regular access to fresh water in a clean dish cannot be overemphasized.

What to Feed Your Puppy

What should you feed your puppy? Although you should initially follow the breeder's advice, you

will eventually settle on a diet of your own choosing. Availability of various brand names may influence your choices. However, the best barometer of what to feed your growing dog is the animal himself. Is he robust and happy? Is his coat shiny? Is his overall healthexcellent? If so, you must be on the right track. Nonetheless, some recommendations based on long experience may prove helpful.

Puppies love to chew, so provide good-quality chew bones—not rawhides or chicken or turkey bones.

About Kibble The mainstay of your puppy's diet—and, indeed, of his adult diet—is the dry food or "kibble" you feed. This food should be advertised on the packaging as "nutritionally complete" or contain some other statement to the same effect. There are as many brand names as there are dog breeds, and making a choice can be confusing.

One of the first things you should learn to do is to *read a dog food packaging label.* Label ingredients are listed in descending order by weight. Therefore, the first item on the list makes up the heaviest volume. If you see chicken or lamb first on the list, however, remember that meat contains up to 75 percent moisture, so it may make up only a small fraction of the entire dry food. The label will go on to list every other component in the food, including minerals, vitamins, and preservatives.

Labels can be misleading, and no reference is made to the actual nutritional value of the ingredients. Nonetheless, you will find that a study of labels can be enlightening to a degree. They vary considerably among manufacturers. In addition to the actual ingredients, the packaging will indicate percentages of protein, fat, fiber, and moisture as contained in the dry food overall. At the present time, according to the American Association of Feed Control Officials (AAFCO), recommended percentages per pound of food for growth are as follows: crude protein, 19.8 percent; crude fat, 7.2 percent.

You will find that most brands of good-quality kibble will meet or exceed the aforementioned percentages. In fact, my own chosen brand of puppy food is made up of 32 percent protein, 21 percent fat, 4 percent fiber, and 10 percent moisture. The amount of dry food you give to your puppy is obviously dependent on the specific brand you use. Manufacturers usually label their foods with suggestions.

How Much to Feed

In general, you will probably feed a growing Boxer puppy (between eight and sixteen weeks of age) between three and four cups of kibble daily. Of course, this amount will vary considerably with the individual puppy's metabolism, his

---

HOW TO READ THE DOG FOOD LABEL

With so many choices on the market, how can you be sure you are feeding the right food for your dog? The information is all there on the label—if you know what you're looking for.

Look for the nutritional claim right up top. Is the food "100% nutritionally complete"? If so, it's for nearly all life stages; "growth and maintenance," on the other hand, is for early development; puppy foods are marked as such, as are foods for senior dogs.

Ingredients are listed in descending order by weight. The first three or four ingredients will tell you the bulk of what the food contains. Look for the highest-quality ingredients, like meats and grains, to be among them.

The Guaranteed Analysis tells you what levels of protein, fat, fiber and moisture are in the food, in that order. While these numbers are meaningful, they won't tell you much about the quality of the food. Nutritional value is in the dry matter, not the moisture content.

In many ways, seeing is believing. If your dog has bright eyes, a shiny coat, a good appetite and a good energy level, chances are his diet's fine. Your dog's breeder and your veterinarian are good sources of advice if you're still confused.

rate of activity, and the amount of any additional foods you may elect to include in his diet. Use your eyes and your common sense. Your puppy should not be fat but rather lean and well-muscled. If you are looking at an animal in optimum condition, you are feeding appropriate foods.

We always feed our kibble soaked briefly in warm water. We begin this practice immediately upon weaning and maintain it throughout the puppy months and adult years. I have always believed that a soaked kibble promotes better digestibility. In addition to water, I usually add a few tablespoons of canned dog food to enhance palatibility—but remember, the greatest nutritional values come from the kibble, not the can! While you could, theoretically, feed your dog nothing but nutritionally complete canned food, most breeders prefer the dry foods. They are also (usually) more economical, and I find that they give a firmer stool— always a consideration when you are picking up after your dog!

Six to Twelve Months of Age

A puppy is offically considered such by the American Kennel Club until she is twelve months old. If you elect to show her, she is eligible to compete in puppy classes from six to twelve months of age. During that transitional time, she is not only growing taller but also beginning to fill out. When your Boxer is ten to twelve months old, you will have some indication of what her adult body type will be. Some dogs mature early, others not until they are older—like people.

Feeding the rapidly growing and maturing puppy presents special challenges. You will be adjusting her food quantity to take into account her general condition and rate of growth. Sooner or later, someone is going to ask you what kind of vitamin-mineral supplement you are including in her diet. We *do not supplement* our growing puppies in pill, capsule or powder form. When our pups reach the age of six months, we discontinue the specially formulated puppy kibble and put them on an excellent-quality adult dry food. This adult kibble contains 23 percent protein and 14 percent fat; yours may differ.

Diet Do's and Don'ts

It is my belief that we can do much more harm than good by tampering with the carefully formulated ingredients in the food we have so conscientiously selected. We are certainly aware, however, that growing puppies need good-quality calcium to promote proper skeletal development. Therefore, I often add foods that are naturally rich in calcium to the pup's routine feedings. These foods include cottage cheese and plain yogurt—easily digested and tasty besides. As long as the pup is an excellent eater, it is perfectly appropriate to offer other naturally good foods; my pups and adults love bananas and cantaloupes!

Many years ago, I sold a young puppy to an intelligent and caring couple. Until I visited them in their home on the opposite coast, I did not realize that their pantry shelves were stocked with every mineral supplement known to man. Not only did they feed these supplements to themselves, they also fed them to their puppy—in great quantities. Not surprisingly, "Chula" developed a skeletal abnormality related to improper levels of calcium and phosphorous. None of her littermates were so afflicted, nor any of her relatives. I thought it a

---

TYPES OF FOODS/TREATS

There are three types of commercially available dog food—dry, canned and semimoist—and a huge assortment of treats (lucky dogs!) to feed your dog. Which should you choose?

Dry and canned foods contain similar ingredients. The primary difference between them is their moisture content. The moisture is not just water. It's blood and broth, too, the very things that dogs adore. So while canned food is more palatable, dry food is more economical, convenient and effective in controlling tartar buildup. Most owners feed a 25% canned/75% dry diet to give their dogs the benefit of both. Just be sure your dog is getting the nutrition he needs (you and your veterinarian can determine this).

Semimoist foods have the flavor dogs love and the convenience owners want. However, they tend to contain excessive amounts of artificial colors and preservatives.

Dog treats come in every size, shape and flavor imaginable, from organic cookies shaped like postmen to beefy chew sticks. Dogs seem to love them all, so enjoy the variety. Just be sure not to overindulge your dog. Factor treats into her regular meal sizes.

lesson well-learned, and I have discouraged all artificial supplementation in puppies from that day to this. You may offer your *adult* dogs any good-quality supplement with relative impunity—but don't overdo!

Good Eating Habits

While you are developing your pup's good eating habits, there are a number of other "Don'ts" to consider. *Do not* feed from your table unless you want a dog annoying you every time you sit down to a meal. What is appealing in a young puppy is decidedly aggravating in an adolescent or an adult weighing fifty to seventy pounds and plopping her paws on your lap while begging with her eyes.

And while we're mentioning table discipline, remember *never* to feed your dog chocolate in any form. A chemical in chocolate (theobromine) is literally poisonous to dogs and can cause death or serious illness.

Many dogs also do not do well with certain "people foods," although they cannot be considered poisonous; for example, I find that my own dogs do not digest potatoes. Others have found spicy foods to disagree with their dogs. You'll know when your dog doesn't take to one of your favorites.

The Adult Boxer

Feeding your adult dog is a matter of maintaining all the good nutritional practices you established when she was a puppy. You will adjust quantities depending on mature physical size and the amount of food you need to maintain your Boxer's good health—and condition—the same way you fed her when she was a puppy. As time goes on, if you are faced with specific medical conditions, your vet may recommend special diets: foods formulated to aid failing kidneys, or volatile intestines, or the geriatric heart.

You will undoubtedly find that the aging dog will need less food than she did in the prime of her life; her metabolism will slow down with the years. Likewise, if your Boxer suffers any tooth loss or gum deterioration as she grows older, you may increase the moisture content of her food so that she finds it easier to swallow.

In conclusion, I think it may be wise to point out that the dog is an omnivore—that is, she eats and utilizes both animal and vegetable matter. Even the wolf and wild dogs of Africa demonstrate this biological fact by first eating the stomachs and intestines of the grass-eating herbivores who make up the mainstay of their natural wild food. Balance in proportion between animal and vegetable matter in the domesticated dog's diet is the key to success in raising a happy and healthy canine, whether it be a Boxer or one of her predacious wild cousins. If you maintain your Boxer on these scientifically formulated and balanced foods, supply her with fresh water for her entire life, and apply common sense liberally, you should find yourself with a healthy, gracefully aging dog who looks younger than her years.

chapter 6

Grooming
Your
Boxer

Grooming your Boxer, as you might imagine, is not a complicated effort. Affectionately known as "wash and wear" dogs, they require no involved grooming procedures. The requirements for keeping your Boxer clean and happy are simple.

You will find it helpful to train your Boxer from puppyhood to stand quietly while you are performing simple grooming tasks. If you are able to work in one particular area, your Boxer will quickly become accustomed to his routine. While it is not necessary, the purchase of a grooming table—a sturdy, non-skid surface on strong metal legs—will be easiest on your own back and eyes, and will tell your Boxer wherever you go that it is time for his regular grooming sessions. These tables fold up and can be easily packed in the car when you are travelling with your dog.

Brushing and Bathing

A Boxer's coat is short and sleek. It is the very devil to remove from clothing and upholstered surfaces, as the little hairs seem to have a willful desire to stick to the most unwelcome places. Your Boxer will shed these hairs with regularity, and if you live in a cold weather area, he will shed almost his entire coat in what will

Boxers don't take naturally to water—good thing they don't need baths too often!

appear like a spring moult! Therefore, a curry comb made of firm rubber, applied in a circular motion, will help you to remove the dead hair coat before it ends up all over you and the upholstery. Be sure that the curry is not too hard and that you apply it gently so as not to irritate his sensitive skin.

Your Boxer will need very few baths in his lifetime. As we have mentioned in Chapter 3, he is a naturally clean animal, licking himself in cat-like fashion to keep himself tidy and polished. Frequent bathing will remove essential oils from your dog's coat and can result in irritation. Any minor surface dirt can be easily whisked away with the use of a soft glove or washcloth. If circumstances demand a bath (for example, your Boxer encountered a fully functioning skunk or decided to roll in cow-pies!) you will want to make sure above all that your dog stays warm throughout the process and does not become chilled. Choose a hot summer day outdoors or a heated bathroom for the procedure. Be sure to dry your dog thoroughly with clean towelling.

When bathing your Boxer, select a mild dog shampoo. If you are bathing to kill fleas, be sure that your veterinarian approves the insecticidal soap you use; some medicated shampoos are toxic not only to the fleas but to the dog as well! First, wet your dog thoroughly with warm water; do not shock him with water either too cold or too hot. Apply your chosen soap conservatively, rub it gently into a lather, and rinse thoroughly. If unrinsed soap dries on your dog's coat, it will look like dandruff and will certainly defeat the purpose for which the Boxer was bathed in the first place!

The "wash and wear" Boxer is an easy dog to keep clean.

Always be careful to avoid getting soap in your dog's eyes. Even if it is not painful to them, it is certainly an irritant. Likewise, try to keep water out of your Boxer's ears—remember, he has no convenient ear "flap" to shed water. If you wish, you can gently swab the inside of the ears with cotton balls dampened with warm water or specially formulated ear cleaner. Do *not* go deep into the ear, as serious damage could be done to the delicate mechanism within.

Trimming Toenails

Regular trimming of your dog's toenails is essential. Untrimmed nails lead to splayed feet and will cause your dog to slip on smooth surfaces. They also look terrible! If you begin gentle trimming on the young puppy, you should have no trouble continuing to trim all through your Boxer's adult life. Your puppy's breeder undoubtedly trimmed nails from the very earliest weeks in the whelping box, so your Boxer may already know the routine.

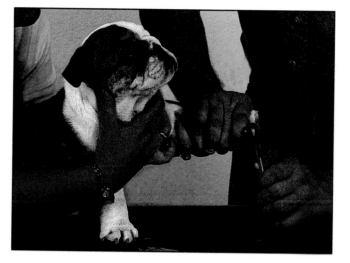

Toenail trimming is necessary, and the sooner your Boxer learns to accept it, the better.

It will help to cut toenails outside on a sunny day. That way, you can hold the nail up to the light and see the quick—the small vein that travels about two-thirds the length of the nail. If you cannot see it, trim off a bit of the nail tip at a time. When the nail begins to look pink inside, stop! Simply try to avoid cutting close to that vein; the area is sensitive, and your dog will tell you if you get too close! In addition to causing momentary discomfort to your dog, an overly aggressive approach will cause transient bleeding. Do not despair; if you make this mistake, you must first apologize to your dog and then dip the nail in some commercially available variant of the familiar styptic powder used by most men who shave their whiskers every morning. In almost every instance, this powder will cause the bleeding to cease almost immediately.

There are several nail-cutting tools available to you. One of these is the familiar "guillotine" type. Another looks like an ordinary scissors designed to fit easily around the nail. Professionals usually choose an

GROOMING TOOLS

pin brush

slicker brush

flea comb

towel

mat rake

grooming glove

scissors

nail clippers

tooth-cleaning equipment

shampoo

conditioner

clippers

electric nail grinder—an expensive but marvelous device. Whatever you choose should be comfortable for you and your Boxer. Be sure to keep blades sharp or replace them as necessary, depending on the tool you have chosen.

Checking Teeth and Gums

Most Boxers do not require regular cleaning of the teeth. However, it is prudent to check them periodi-

cally, just to be sure that there are no injuries to the enamel or to the gums. If your dog's mouth is "smelly," he probably does need attention. It means retained and decaying food is stuck in his teeth and causing the stink. You can gently brush your Boxer's teeth with a soft human toothbrush, or a canine brush available at pet supply stores. You can

Done on a table, a thorough grooming session is easy to accomplish.

use baking soda and water or one of the commercially available canine toothpastes. Do not be alarmed if you see an overgrowth of gum tissue in the older Boxer; this is most probably a benign condition rather common to the breed (see "Gingival Hyperplasia" in Chapter 7).

If your Boxer has regular access to rubber, nylon or rope chew toys, and if he gets occasional hard-baked food treats (biscuits), you will usually find that the simple stimulus of chewing will keep his mouth and teeth healthy, and that tartar deposits remain at a minimum.

If you elect to exhibit your Boxer in competitive conformation shows, grooming will take on another dimension. Although the procedure will still be relatively simple, some additional measures will be needed. These include the trimming of the facial whiskers with a scissors or electric trimmer, shaving the inside of the ears to present a sharper appearance, and shaving the underside of the tail and trimming the end to look neat. Any stray hairs should also be trimmed from the end of the penile sheath in males, and, likewise, unwanted hairs on the belly of either sex should be gently shaved. Be careful with clippers: if you make a cosmetic mistake, it will be very visible on your short-haired Boxer and will take some time to grow out.

A rubber curry comb works well on Boxers. This pup is being trained to enjoy grooming.

As you can see, grooming your Boxer is not complicated, but regular attention to his appearance will help to ensure his good health. You will find that these grooming sessions will be pleasurable for both you and your dog.

chapter 7

Keeping Your
Boxer
Healthy

I hope you will have the privilege of your Boxer's company for many years. While not so long-lived as some breeds, Boxers, with good care, commonly live ten to twelve or more years. When health problems do arise, your dog's best line of defense is *you*—the loving, alert owner who will see to it that proper medical treatment is rendered early and effectively.

Choosing a Veterinarian

You will find that your choice of veterinarian is critical to your dog's good care. This practitioner must not only be skilled as a diagnostician and a surgeon, but must also be a good listener—to you, as you know your dog best. Beware the vet who never has time to talk to you, or doesn't care what you have to say. Beware the vet who constantly belittles your medical expertise. The best medical professionals will be acutely interested in your observations and your insights. Seek recommendations from experienced breeders in your area; they will offer very definite opinions on who you should trust to do the right thing in a time of crisis. They may know that a particular vet has a particular knowledge of or love for the Boxer breed. All this advice is helpful, but the final choice is yours. Be sure you have confidence in your vet, that he or she is medically skilled and is someone to whom you can relate.

Preventive Health Care

Your Boxer's first line of defense against illness is you, the care-giver who sees him daily. You must be alert to any signs that would indicate a deviation from the usual state of health. Often, sometimes before your veterinarian can make a definitive

Check your dog's teeth frequently and brush them regularly.

diagnosis of trouble, you may notice subtle changes that would escape the notice of anyone else. Perhaps your Boxer seems slightly less enthusiastic about his food, seems to be drinking more water than usual, or just doesn't want to engage in his usual play activities. Trust your instincts; follow up on your suspicions with a closer look, and if your dog does not quickly resume his normal behavior patterns, seek professional help.

VACCINATIONS

When you purchased your puppy, he undoubtedly already had one or more vaccinations. These shots are administered to prevent certain communicable diseases, and are manufactured in either killed or modified live virus form. They stimulate your puppy to produce antibodies to the specific disease for which they are formulated. You will need to keep a careful record of all your pup's shots, and you should embark on an immunization program in consultation with your veterinarian. Do not delay this consultation. The timing is critical, and in addition to puppy shots, your adult Boxer will undoubtedly need yearly boosters to keep his immunity up-to-date. (A discussion of the infectious diseases dogs are vaccinated against begins on page 82.)

ADVANTAGES OF SPAY/NEUTER

The greatest advantage of spaying (for females) or neutering (for males) your dog is that you are guaranteed your dog will not produce puppies. There are too many puppies already available for too few homes. There are other advantages as well.

ADVANTAGES OF SPAYING

No messy heats.

No "suitors" howling at your windows or waiting in your yard.

Decreased incidences of pyometra (disease of the uterus) and breast cancer.

ADVANTAGES OF NEUTERING

Lessens male aggressive and territorial behaviors, but doesn't affect the dog's personality. Behaviors are often owner-induced, so neutering is not the only answer, but it is a good start.

Prevents the need to roam in search of bitches in season.

Decreased incidences of urogenital diseases.

SPAYING AND NEUTERING

The pet population explosion is rampant. We have all been assailed in the media by the pathetic photos of unwanted pets, and the harsh statistics that indicate so many thousands being euthanized yearly. Unless you have specifically purchased your Boxer for breeding, you will undoubtedly want to spay her or neuter him. Not only will the procedure prevent your female from coming into season and attracting all the neighborhood canine lotharios, but it may also make your male more of a homebody and will curb his interest in the opposite sex. In addition, there is considerable medical evidence that certain kinds of reproductive cancers are virtually eliminated in dogs who have undergone early sterilization procedures. You should consult your vet for specific recommendations. (Also see the sidebar at left.)

ROUTINE CHECKUPS

It is sound medical advice to take your Boxer to the veterinarian for routine examinations—every six months in an aging dog, or at least every year for a normal dog. The professional will listen to your dog's heart for any irregularities and will check him thoroughly. He may pick up an abnormality apparent to only his professional eyes and ears. Fecal checks for internal parasites can also be run at this time.

Home Health Care

TAKING YOUR DOG'S TEMPERATURE

One of the most important items you should own is a simple rectal thermometer. While a normal temperature is not necessarily an indicator of good health, an elevated or subnormal temperature may indicate certain deleterious conditions. Your Boxer's normal temperature will be in the range of 100.5° to 102.5° F. Any routine call to your vet for help should include a fresh reading of your dog's temperature.

Taking this reading is quite simple. Lubricate the end of the thermometer with some petroleum jelly so that it can be inserted gently into the rectum. Leave it in place for a minute or two. Keep a string attached to it or hold onto it while it's inside your dog so that it is not drawn in to the dog and you can't get it out. After two minutes, withdraw it, wipe it off and read it. Your Boxer may find the process slightly uncomfortable, but most dogs will allow you to perform your task without serious protest.

FIRST-AID EQUIPMENT

Your canine medicine cabinet should contain gauze pads and cloth bandages—all to be used in either

A FIRST-AID KIT

Keep a canine first-aid kit on hand for general care and emergencies. Check it periodically to make sure liquids haven't spilled or dried up, and replace medications and materials after they're used. Your kit should include:

Activated charcoal tablets

Adhesive tape
(1 and 2 inches wide)

Antibacterial ointment
(for skin and eyes)

Aspirin (buffered or enteric coated, *not* Ibuprofen)

Bandages: Gauze rolls (1 and 2 inches wide) and dressing pads

Cotton balls

Diarrhea medicine

Dosing syringe

Hydrogen peroxide (3%)

Petroleum jelly

Rectal thermometer

Rubber gloves

Rubbing alcohol

Scissors

Tourniquet

Towel

Tweezers

routine or emergency situations. Be sure you know where these items are so that you can use them quickly if the situation warrants. Make certain that one of the bandage strips can serve as a muzzle if you need to apply it. (See "Handling an Injured Dog" later in this chapter.)

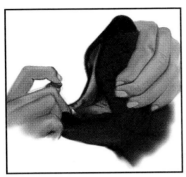

To give a pill, open the mouth wide, then drop it in the back of the throat.

Simple tweezers, adhesive tape, antiseptic, germicidal soaps, antibacterial ointments, ipecac and cotton balls are helpful items to have on hand. Ask your veterinarian for specific recommendations if you have questions, and see the sidebar on page 73 for other items you should have on hand.

Do not purchase over-the-counter preparations without checking with your vet first; some of these may be dangerous to your Boxer. They include, but are not limited to, aspirin and other analgesics, "worm" medicines, and flea/tick products.

GIVING MEDICATION

Squeeze eye ointment into the lower lid.

You can hide pills in hamburger or another tasty treat and feed them easily to most Boxers. Failing that, you

can open the dog's jaws with one hand while pushing the pill gently down the gullet with the other. Massage the throat to encourage swallowing, and make sure that the dog does not spit out the medicine.

Liquid preparations can be squirted carefully and slowly into the rear side pocket formed by the Boxer's pendulous lips. Open the jaws with one hand, raise the head slightly, and administer the liquid.

To apply eye ointment or drops, face your dog and carefully pull down the lower eyelid. This action will cause a "pocket" to form between the lid and the eyeball. Squeeze or drip the appropriate medication into this pocket, and release the lower lid. The medication will be dispersed over the surface of the eye.

Emergencies

Your dog's normal heart rate should be 70 to 160 beats per minute. Her respiratory rate should be 10 to 30 breaths per minute (at rest), and her normal rectal temperature, 100.5 to 102.5 degrees F. If your dog has been in a serious accident, or encountered a serious trauma, you must first analyze the situation at hand. Ask yourself these questions:

- Is your Boxer bleeding profusely?

- Are her gums pale and white, indicating shock or internal bleeding?

- Is there any obvious abnormality such as a broken limb, severe contusions, or an obstructed airway?

The ability to assess these conditions quickly will enable you to perform what could be life-saving emergency care.

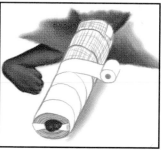

Make a temporary splint by wrapping the leg in firm casing, then bandaging it.

Bleeding

If blood is spurting from the dog in rhythmic bursts, an artery has undoubtedly been cut. Whether the wound involves an artery or a major vein, you must act quickly. Applying a tourniquet is a good idea, but putting direct pressure on the wound may be a faster and more effective treatment. You can use a pressure bandage, or your hand, or whatever works with whatever is available. If you apply a tourniquet, which you can make by tearing off a strip of your clothing if nothing else is available, place it above the wound, wrap it and pull it tight until the bleeding stops or lessens dramatically. You must be very careful with tourniquets: Whereas they may save your dog's life, they also cut off circulation to the affected area, and should be used with caution.

EMERGENCY RESUSCITATION

If a dog is in danger of death from suffocation, you must immediately restore his airway if it is blocked. If he has been underwater and has stopped breathing, lift him by his hindquarters so that his head and neck hang vertical—you are trying to drain fluids from his lungs. If you cannot lift him, lie him on his side so that his head is lower than his body and fluids can drain out.

For **CPR** (Cardiopulmonary Resuscitation), clear the mouth of mucus and draw the tongue forward. Place both hands, one on top of the other, over the region of the heart—where the elbow meets the ribs. Compress the chest by vigorous downward thrusts, about 100 compressions per minute. Check for a heartbeat about every thirty seconds.

CHECKING FOR A PULSE

The easiest way to check to see whether the heart is beating is by feeling for the femoral arterial pulse on the inside of your Boxer's upper rear legs. If you move your index finger down the femur (upper bone) and apply slight pressure, you should easily be able to feel the pulse.

ARTIFICIAL RESPIRATION

Exhaled air contains about 16 percent oxygen. This small amount is enough to sustain life in both people and dogs. Although the Boxer's short muzzle and nasal passages present special difficulties, mouth-to-muzzle breathing can be accomplished by closing the muzzle with one hand and placing your mouth over your dog's nostrils and exhaling. Remember to keep the head extended. Watch your dog's chest: If he is getting air into his lungs, you will see a slight rise and fall as you breathe the air into him. Administering ten to fifteen rapid rib thrusts and one deep breath—repeated until help can arrive or you can get to a vet—will give your dog a chance. If the chest does not rise and fall, and you feel the nasal passages are blocked, try sealing the nose and breathing directly into the mouth. Your task will be much easier if two people are available—one to perform CPR and one to employ artificial respiration. A ratio of one to four breaths to chest compressions is ideal.

These tasks are physically demanding—it is genuinely hard labor—but do not despair and do not give up until ten to fifteen minutes have passed with no response from your dog.

CHOKING

If your dog is choking or unconscious after unsuccessful efforts to cough up a foreign object, you must attempt the canine equivalent of the Heimlich maneuver. First, if you are able, reach deep into the throat to try to pull the object out. If you succeed

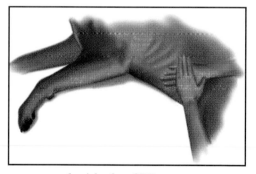

Applying abdominal thrusts can save a choking dog.

and the dog is not breathing, proceed with the CPR and artificial respiration techniques just outlined. If you do *not* succeed in removing the object, lie the dog on his side and place your palms, one on top of the other, on the abdomen right below the rib cage. Administer a sharp, upward thrust to this area and repeat until the object is expelled. If these efforts fail, proceed with CPR.

HANDLING AN INJURED DOG

If your Boxer is in pain, no matter how much he loves you, he may bite if you try to handle him. Therefore,

*Use a scarf or
old hose to
make a tempo-
rary muzzle, as
shown.*

wind a strip of cloth (a stocking will do) around his muzzle, in back of the nose, and tie it in a half-knot. Make a second closed loop, and pull so that it is under the jaw. Complete the procedure by tying a tight bow behind the ears. A muzzle will prevent the real potential of injury to you. If a blanket is available, try to slide it under your dog and carry him to safety or into your car for a trip to the vet. Your coat or a sweater may take the place of a blanket in an emergency. Try not to jostle the dog.

SHOCK

Shock is a generalized, progressive failure of the circulatory system, usually due to trauma or overwhelming infection. Common signs of shock include labored breathing; a weak, rapid pulse; pale gums; cold extremities; and eventual coma. Anytime your Boxer has suffered a severe trauma, he is in danger from shock and must be seen by a veterinarian immediately. Sometimes the shock syndrome can prove fatal even if the initial trauma is not. Treatment involves intravenous fluids and other appropriate professional therapy. Be sure to keep your dog warm until medical help is available. Unless absolutely necessary, do not muzzle a dog in shock; his breathing may be too restricted.

HEATSTROKE

The short muzzle of the Boxer renders him particularly susceptible to heatstroke. He must never be left in a closed car in hot weather—even briefly. The interior of an unventilated automobile can become a death trap in just a few minutes. Even with the windows open, a Boxer is at risk. Likewise, he must not be left outside in the sun without shelter, nor permitted too much strenuous physical activity on hot days. Use your common sense.

Signs of heatstroke are related to very high internal temperature—even up to 109° F—a reading that will result in rapid death if the condition is not treated immediately. The dog with heatstroke will have a weak and rapid pulse, pale and often greyish gums, warm and dry skin. Some dogs vomit and have diarrhea.

If your dog is experiencing heatstroke, rapid cooling is in order. This can be accomplished with a cold water bath, or by hosing him down. If he does not improve in a few minutes (ideally, check the rectal temperature), you may give him a cold water enema, but rectal temperature readings will not be accurate if this procedure is performed.

Get your dog to a veterinarian immediately so that he may receive additional treatment. But remember—get your Boxer's temperature down without delay. Speed is essential.

POISONING

The National Animal Poison Control Center operates a twenty-four-hour hotline to call should you suspect your dog has been poisoned. The number is (800) 548-2423. Post it somewhere convenient so that you have ready access in an emergency. Your dog may be poisoned by a variety of substances, some obvious and some quite unexpected.

Run your hands regularly over your dog to feel for any injuries.

The symptoms of poisoning are as varied as the toxic agent ingested. They may include nausea, vomiting, bleeding from bodily orifices, seizures, convulsions, salivation, labored breathing and collapse. No matter what time of day or night the poisoning occurs, call your veterinarian immediately. He or she may tell you to induce vomiting. One teaspoon of ipecac per ten pounds of body weight, up to a maximum of one

*Some of the
many house-
hold substances
harmful to your
dog.*

tablespoon, should prove effective. If ipecac is unavailable, one teaspoon of hydrogen peroxide (3 percent strength or less) per ten pounds, or one tablespoon per thirty pounds, may be substituted. Certain poisons, such as caustic lye and petroleum products, should *not* be vomited. That is why you should always consult your veterinarian.

Remember that many **plants** are poisonous to your dog. These include yew, amaryllis, nightshade, monkshood, daffodil bulbs and a host of others.

Household products such as shoe polish, mothballs, paint, dye, turpentine, antifreeze, and suntan lotion are toxic. Many lawn fertilizers and weed killers are poisonous and can be ingested through licking them off the paws. Years ago a friend sold a healthy puppy who was dead in a few days because the lawn had been treated with chlordane. **Chocolate** is poisonous to dogs and even in small amounts can prove fatal. If in doubt call your vet and/or the hotline. Speed is often critical.

BLOAT

This condition may prove to be a life-threatening emergency. The stomach distends with gas and air, and you may observe that suddenly your Boxer's abdomen looks very full and abnormally large. The dog may whine, salivate, and make unsuccessful attempts to vomit. Unfortunately, this distension often causes the stomach to twist on its axis (torsion), cutting off its circulation. Shock and death follow without surgical intervention.

In simple bloat, without torsion, the condition may be relieved by the passage of a stomach tube to release the gaseous pressure.

Bloat and torsion are often associated with the rapid ingestion of a large meal or too much water, and vigorous exercise before or after eating or drinking.

However, some dogs develop bloat for unknown reasons. It is prudent to feed your Boxer two meals a day so that he does not eat a huge quantity at any one time. We usually restrict exercise for at least one hour after a meal. The frantic gulping of food, which necessitates the ingestion of a large amount of air, should be discouraged. If you suspect bloat and/or torsion, do not waste time getting to your vet.

Common Infectious Diseases

Despite our best efforts, our dogs do occasionally contract serious diseases. Sometimes vaccines fail, though this is a relatively rare occurrence; sometimes we fail to remember the necessary yearly booster shots. The following descriptions should help you recognize some of the more common infectious diseases. The immunization program your veterinarian will schedule for your dog should protect against all of them.

CORONAVIRUS

A highly contagious gastrointestinal viral disease, coronavirus is most severe in the young puppy. Signs include vomiting, diarrhea, fever, and depression. Corona often comes on quite suddenly. Treatment includes the replacement of depleted fluids and appropriate antibiotics—often to control secondary infections. Coronavirus is sensitive to most disinfectants, especially preparations containing common household bleach. Scrupulous sanitation will help to eliminate the virus from the premises. It would be wise to avoid dog shows and visits to outside kennels while your puppy is being immunized.

> ### YOUR PUPPY'S VACCINES
>
> Vaccines are given to prevent your dog from getting an infectious disease like canine distemper or rabies. Vaccines are the ultimate preventive medicine: they're given before your dog ever gets the disease so as to protect him from the disease. That's why it is necessary for your dog to be vaccinated routinely. Puppy vaccines start at eight weeks of age for the five-in-one DHLPP vaccine and are given every three to four weeks until the puppy is sixteen months old. Your veterinarian will put your puppy on a proper schedule and will remind you when to bring in your dog for shots.

DISTEMPER

This systemic viral disease is highly contagious. The dog will usually develop a fever three to six days after infection. This fever subsides for several days, but a second fever follows. A dog with distemper looks like she has a cold: There is usually a mucous discharge from both nose and eyes. Also, white blood cell count is lowered; gastrointestinal and respiratory problems may occur; the pads of the feet may appear to be thickened and hard; and central nervous system complications may occur simultaneously with the other symptoms, or may follow the acute clinical disease. The central nervous system symptoms include spasms, seizures, or paralysis. Distemper is often fatal. Treatment involves good nursing care, fluid replacement, and antibiotics to cure secondary infections.

Your Boxers love to play, but be careful of chipping teeth, insect bites and other injuries. Check your dogs when you get inside.

HEPATITIS

This acute viral infection can produce anything from slight fever to death. It most commonly kills very young puppies. Signs include fever, rapid heartbeat, general depression, thirst, mucous discharge from eyes and nose, bloody diarrhea, and prolonged blood-clotting time. Organs affected include the liver, pancreas, and kidney. Onset is abrupt. A dog with hepatitis may require blood transfusions and antibiotics.

Infectious Tracheobronchitis ("Kennel Cough")

This disease is usually mild and self-limiting. The upper respiratory passages are inflamed, and the infection results in a harsh, dry, gagging cough of sudden onset. Coughing can be elicited by pressure over the trachea. Appetite is usually normal or only slightly depressed. Temperature remains near normal. Treatment is aimed at controlling any secondary infections that may develop, including pneumonia. Young pups are most severely affected. Kennel cough is highly contagious and will often move rapidly through an entire kennel or household. Immunization may not entirely prevent your dog from getting the disease but will greatly lessen its severity should your dog become infected.

Your Boxer should get a checkup at least every year.

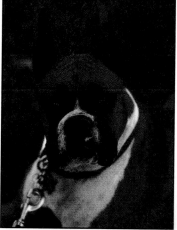

Leptospirosis

This is an acute infection usually acquired from contact with affected urine, often that of rodents. It is contagious to man, so treatment of affected dogs must include scrupulous hygiene. Initial symptoms include bloody diarrhea, vomiting, fever between 103° and 105° F, loss of appetite, and generalized weakness. Thirst becomes marked as the disease progresses, and the dog's temperature may fall to subnormal. The dog may be unwilling to rise and may exhibit signs of pain in the back and abdomen. As time progresses, the eyes become sunken in the head, swallowing becomes difficult, and saliva may become tinged with blood. If death ensues, it is usually due to kidney infection and eventual failure, usually five to ten days after symptoms appear. Treatment includes antibiotics and fluids.

Parvovirus

Parvo is an acute viral infection, often fatal to pups under twelve weeks of age. It manifests as two different forms of disease: enteritis (intestinal inflammation) and myocarditis (inflammation of the heart muscle). Symptoms include vomiting, hemorrhagic diarrhea, lethargy, rapid dehydration, and fever. Death may be sudden. Treatment includes antibiotics, restoration of fluids, and intensive nursing care. Parvo is highly contagious.

RABIES

Just the name of this disease strikes fear into the hearts of pet owners. It's an acute viral infection that afflicts all warm-blooded animals. The death rate approaches 100 percent. Transmission of the disease is usually

Dogs get round-worms by eating infected soil or feces: Keep your yard clean!

through the saliva of an infected animal that has bitten its victim. The incubation period can be as long as eighty days in the dog. Symptoms are manifested in two forms of the disease: the "dumb" form, characterized by paralysis of the throat, dropping of the lower jaw, and extreme passivity; and the "furious" form, where the dog is visciously aggressive and loses all fear. Dogs rarely survive ten days after symptoms become evident. Rabies is definitively diagnosed by examining fresh brain tissue after death. Most states mandate vaccination for rabies, and the vaccines must be kept current.

Internal Parasites

A variety of internal parasites can infect your Boxer, both as a puppy and as an adult. Fortunately, many can be prevented by scrupulous attention to hygiene. If your dog does become afflicted, there are effective, safe medications to eliminate the parasite from your pet. Remember—most of these medications are *potentially* toxic; they must be dosed with care. This warning includes the so-called "all-natural" preparations.

Always consult your veterinarian for proper drugs of choice and *do not* casually administer over-the-counter remedies. Fecal examinations are utilized to identify any specific parasite; therefore, routine checks are advisable.

ROUNDWORMS (ASCARIDS)

This is a common parasite, especially in puppies. Signs of infection include a failure to thrive, dull coat, and "pot-belly" appearance. Your dog may come down with mucuslike diarrhea and pneumonia (due to migrating larvae in the lungs). Roundworm eggs are ingested by eating infected soil and feces, and can be transmitted to people. Despite all a breeder's best efforts, many pups are born with a roundworm infection acquired from the mother before the pup is born.

It is not uncommon to see roundworms in your dog's stool. They are "stringy" and white, and may be elongated or coiled. In severe infestations, a puppy may vomit the worms. Since an adult female roundworm may lay 200,000 eggs daily, early detection and elimination are essential.

> ### WHEN TO CALL THE VET
>
> In any emergency situation, you should call your veterinarian immediately. You can make the difference in your dog's life by staying as calm as possible when you call and by giving the doctor or the assistant as much information as possible before you leave for the clinic. That way, the vet will be able to take immediate, specific action to remedy your dog's situation.
>
> Emergencies include acute abdominal pain, suspected poisoning, snakebite, burns, frostbite, shock, dehydration, abnormal vomiting or bleeding, and deep wounds. You are the best judge of your dog's health, as you live with and observe him every day. Don't hesitate to call your veterinarian if you suspect trouble.

HOOKWORMS

These live in the small intestine and exert their influence on the host by attaching to the intestinal wall and sucking blood. As they move to new feeding sites, the old wounds they have caused ulcerate and continue to bleed. Thus, a puppy heavily infected with hookworms may develop a profound anemia. Pale gums; dark, tarry diarrhea; weakness; and emaciation are all clinical signs. Transfusions may be necessary in severe infestations. Adult dogs may harbor a chronic infection with less dramatic symptoms.

TAPEWORMS

These parasites are transmitted to the dog via the intermediate host, the flea. They can be up to seventy centimeters long, and segments resembling grains of rice may be passed in the feces. Tapeworms cause general unthriftiness, colic, mild diarrhea and occasional inappetance. Flea control is important to interrupt the life cycle of the worm.

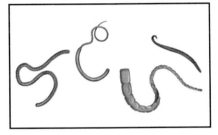

Common internal parasites (l-r): roundworm, whipworm, tapeworm and hookworm.

WHIPWORMS

These are sometimes difficult to detect in fecal exams because they shed their eggs intermittently. Repeated testing may be necessary. Adult whipworms live in the cecum, a pouch in the large intestine. Signs in a light infestation are minimal, but severe infections produce weight loss, a poor coat, and diarrhea often streaked with fresh blood. Whipworm eggs will not survive in dry areas, and regular cleaning of any moist spots in the yard or kennel run will help to control infections.

HEARTWORM

This is a serious disease that is often fatal without treatment. The worm itself is transmitted in larval form by the bite of infected mosquitoes. Adult worms live in the heart muscle itself and cause symptoms related to circulatory disturbances. These include weakness, coughing, intolerance to exercise, respiratory distress, weight loss and sudden death. Heartworm disease can be prevented by daily or monthly doses of appropriate medication throughout the mosquito season and for two months thereafter. Before beginning any heartworm medication, your dog must get a bloodtest to check that there are no worms in his system already. In some parts of the country, veterinarians advise that dogs be kept on heartworm preventive year-round.

COCCIDIA

Coccidia are protozoan parasites living in the intestines. They most commonly affect puppies. Symptoms include bloody diarrhea, emaciation and dehydration. Proper sanitation is critical, and certain sulfa drugs are curative.

GIARDIA

This protozoal disease infects mammals and birds. The parasites live in the small intestine and are transmitted via the feces of the host. Symptoms include chronic diarrhea, which may be intermittent, as well as weight loss. The feces are pale and may contain mucous.

External Parasites

FLEAS

A flea is a bloodsucking insect. It carries disease and acts as an intermediate host to the tapeworm. It can jump great distances and readily attaches itself to a host if one is available. Fleas need moisture and warmth to grow and multiply; therefore, in seasonal climates they often do not pose a problem in the winter. In tropical climates or in heated interiors, they can be a problem all year long.

Flea bites cause local irritation; hence, your dog will scratch in an attempt to rid himself of these parasites. Some dogs are allergic to the saliva in fleabites and develop an acute hypersensitivity to fleas. They exhibit signs related to intense itching, and will constantly scratch and bite where fleas have bitten them. This self-mutilation can be a serious problem, and even a very few fleas can cause this severe flea allergy dermatitis.

Fleas are prodigious multipliers and may seem to be everywhere. Female fleas lay eggs that drop off and hatch into larvae resembling worms. These larvae become adult fleas. Unchecked, they may make your home unlivable, and will readily feed on you if you send your dog on a vacation.

Fleas are easy to see. They look like small, dark, moving specks. If the infection is slight, you may see only "flea dirt" on your Boxer's short coat. These tiny specks look like bits of dirt, but they're actually flea feces. If you moisten them, you will see the water become tinged red, as they contain blood. Common sites of infestation are at the scrotum and around and under the tail. In serious infections, fleas may be found anywhere on the dog.

There are no easy solutions to controlling fleas. Not only the dog but also his environment must be treated. Insecticidal shampoos for the dog; foggers, sprays, or bombs (preferably containing insect growth regulators to prevent larvae from developing into mature insects) for the environment; soaps and powders—all may be used to effect. Remember, however, that all of these products contain toxic chemicals and must be used with caution. Always consult your veterinarian for professional advice. Pay particular attention to medications affecting young puppies. I, personally, do not use flea collars, although they may be safe and effective if carefully monitored.

FIGHTING FLEAS

Remember, the fleas you see on your dog are only part of the problem—the smallest part! To rid your dog and home of fleas, you need to treat your dog *and* your home. Here's how:

• Identify where your pet(s) sleep. These are "hot spots."

• Clean your pets' bedding regularly by vacuuming and washing.

• Spray "hot spots" with a non-toxic, long-lasting flea larvicide.

• Treat outdoor "hot spots" with insecticide.

• Kill eggs on pets with a product containing insect growth regulators (IGRs).

• Kill fleas on pets per your veterinarian's recommendation.

TICKS

Ticks are bloodsucking parasites. They are discouragingly hardy and are carriers for many diseases, including Rocky Mountain spotted fever, Lyme disease and encephalitis. They are found outdoors in high grass and wooded areas, and are adept at locating your dog. They can attach themselves anywhere but have a preference for the inside of the ears. You may first notice them if your Boxer seems to be scratching at one particular site. In addition, Boxers seem to have a specific skin

sensitivity to certain tick bites: Ticks native to my New England area cause a raised welt around the bite, which is often my first warning of the tick embedded therein.

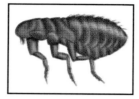

The flea is a die-hard pest.

Ticks may be manually removed with tweezers or pulled out with gloved hands. It is not necessary to burn them with a match. Just be sure to grasp the tick close to the skin and pull straight out so as not to leave the head. Swab the area with disinfectant, and wash your hands thoroughly. During the tick "season," which can be anytime the temperature is above freezing, you should do a daily exam for ticks on your Boxer. Tick control products are available for the dog and the environment. As with those for fleas, consult your veterinarian and heed the potential toxicities of these chemicals.

LYME DISEASE

This tickborne disease is widespread throughout the U.S. It is caused by a spirochete, *Borrelia burgdorferi*, and transmitted primarily by the deer tick, though it's suspected that other ticks may carry the spirochete as well. Intermediate hosts include deer, mice, and other rodents. Symptoms are usually of rapid onset. They

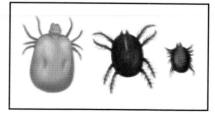

include depression, fever in the range of 103° to 105° F, inappetance, joint swelling, and often severe pain in the limbs and/or back. This pain may migrate from one site to another.

Three types of ticks (l-r): the wood tick, brown dog tick and deer tick.

Not all symptoms will appear in an individual case, and thus Lyme is difficult to diagnose and is often mistaken for other problems. Your veterinarian must be alert to the possibility of Lyme in your area and take appropriate measures. These include blood testing for the disease; however, a negative titre does not necessarily mean Lyme is to be ruled out. Antibiotic therapy early in the course of infection will cure most cases of Lyme Disease, but misdiagnosis and lack of appropriate treatment can eventually lead to fatal complications. Unfortunately, successful treatment does not bring immunity, and your Boxer will be susceptible again if she is bitten by an infected tick.

Use tweezers to remove ticks from your dog.

Medical Conditions Specific to Boxers

Despite all our care and attention, our Boxers do occasionally suffer from conditions to which the breed seems to be predisposed. Whether these illnesses are genetic in origin or occasioned by environmental factors, they nonetheless need to be addressed.

CANCER

Boxers have been found to be at high risk for a large variety of tumors. These include both benign skin tumors (lipomas and histiocytomas) as well as cancers affecting the brain, skin, thyroid, mammary glands and testes, and internal organs such as the spleen and pancreas. Benign skin tumors usually need either no treatment or simple surgical removal under local anesthesia. Malignancies require treatment specific to the cancer itself and vary widely. As in human cancers, dogs are treated with surgery, chemotherapy, and sometimes radiation. There have been tremendous advances made in canine treatment and survival times. There is no way to predict whether your Boxer will develop any cancer as he ages. However, it is prudent to be alert to any unusual medical developments and consult with your veterinarian if you observe anything suspicious.

Gingival Hyperplasia

These are benign tumors of the mouth, mainly an overgrowth of gum tissue, commonly seen in middle-aged and older Boxers. These tumors may be numerous; however, they usually cause no significant harm. Occasionally, they distort the placement of the lips and are cosmetically unattractive. Since they may catch and hold food particles, the owner must pay attention to oral hygiene. Always consult your veterinarian to rule out any potential malignancy.

Heart Disease

Like most breeds of dogs, Boxers are subject to heart ailments. These include congenital anomalies as well as acquired disease later in life. Boxer heart disease usually falls into two categories: aortic stenosis and cardiomyopathy.

Aortic stenosis is a congenital condition, a narrowing or constriction of the outflow tract from the left ventricle to the aorta. Usually, this defect occurs below the aortic valve and thus is referred to as subaorticstenosis (SAS). It can be detected as a systolic murmur by your veterinarian—often in a young puppy if the narrowing is severe, or in an older dog if the constriction is less acute. This murmur must be distinguished from other types of murmurs—often so-called innocent "flow" murmurs that disappear as a puppy grows. There is no practical surgical treatment, and if the condition results in ventricular arrhythmias, anti-arrhythmic therapy is usually instituted. SAS can cause heart failure and/or sudden death, but mild forms of the anomaly may go undetected and are not incompatible with a normal life span.

Cardiomyopathy is a disease of the heart muscle itself. It causes life-threatening arrhythmias and often leads to sudden death or heart failure. It can be caused by certain poisons; bacterial, parasitic, and viral infections (notably parvovirus); severe uremia; diabetes; and heatstroke. In Boxers, however, it often occurs in middle age due to no known disease entity. Undoubtedly, heredity plays a key role.

Cardiomyopathy is widespread throughout the breed in North America, and there are no easy ways to avoid it. The good news is that there is an excellent chance that your Boxer will never develop this condition. Nonetheless, you must be aware of its symptoms. If your Boxer ever displays a sudden weakness, or faints, you must investigate the cause of this behavior. These are classic cardiomyopathy symptoms in the breed, and they must not be ignored. Often, if you take your dog to the vet after such an episode, her heart rhythm may be normal. Unfortunately, this is no guarantee of a healthy heart, because arrhythmias, usually ventricular in origin, may only be detected upon stress in early stages of the disease. More sophisticated testing is required.

An Elizabethan collar keeps your dog from licking a fresh wound.

Cardiomyopathy can be treated with antiarrhythmic drugs, and once a dog's heart is properly regulated, she may live for years with no further symptoms. Conscientious Boxer breeders are funding research into this problem and hope one day to identify genetic "markers" so that cardiomyopathy can eventually be eliminated or greatly reduced in the breeding population.

HIP DYSPLASIA

This is a developmental disease of the hip joint affecting many breeds of dogs, including Boxers. The head of the femur (thigh bone) and the acetabulum (hip socket) become incompatible; the joint weakens and loses proper function. Reluctance to engage in strenuous physical activity, lameness and pain are all possible signs of hip dysplasia, usually manifested between the ages of four months to one year. Stair climbing or rising from a sitting or lying position may be difficult, and the dog may cry out if the hip joint is manipulated. Radiographs are definitively diagnostic and will show evidence of abnormal joint laxity. Treatment is aimed at relieving symptoms of pain and includes drug therapy and surgery. Hip dysplasia is believed to be hereditary, but other factors such as diet and conditioning cannot be ruled out. Dogs older than twenty-four months can be evaluated by and registered with the Orthopedic Foundation for Animals (OFA) in Columbia, Missouri (see Chapter 13 for the address).

HYPOTHYROIDISM (THYROID DEFICIENCY)

The onset of hypothyroidism in the adult Boxer is becoming more commonly diagnosed. Hypothyroidism may be caused by thyroid tumors or a primary malfunction of the gland. What happens is the thyroid gland proves to be deficient in the production of thyroid hormones. The deficient thyroid may have an effect on many organ systems, including the heart. Symptoms may include excessive hair thinning and loss, obesity, anemia, reproductive failures and infertility, and lethargy. Diagnosis is confirmed by testing the blood and confirming inadequate levels of circulating thyroid hormones. The administration of carefully determined doses of replacement hormone will alleviate most symptoms and will probably need to be given for the balance of the dog's life.

Older Boxers, like people, turn gray and have trouble hearing and seeing as well as they once did.

The Aging Boxer

Canine geriatric medicine has made great advances over the years. Full and happy lives can often be prolonged by appropriate medical treatments designed to rejuvenate and relieve the stress from failing organ systems. The elder Boxer is a great gift—a treasured friend who has shared and enriched your family member's lives for many years.

Symptoms of Aging

While most Boxers tend to act youthful all their lives, your elder statesman may decline to run and play as he once did. He may develop arthritis; if he suffered any skeletal or joint injuries in his life, they may begin to cause him discomfort. He may have difficulty rising or exhibit intermittent lameness. There are excellent pain remedies for these problems that can be prescribed by your veterinarian.

Your own responsibilities to the geriatric dog are mostly a matter of good common sense. He should not be allowed to become obese. Extra weight in dogs, as in people, puts undue stress on the heart and skeletal system. As your Boxer ages, his metabolism will slow and he will require fewer calories. There are excellent foods carefully formulated for the older dog. If your Boxer seems inclined to tear around as if he were a puppy, but you know that he has a fragile knee joint or spinal arthritis or a bad heart, limit his exercise within sensible parameters. Give him a nice soft bed to lie on. And above all, keep up his grooming, keep his toenails trimmed, and make him feel that he is still a valued member of the household.

Saying Good-bye

When the time comes to say good-bye, you may be lucky enough to find your old friend has left you as if dreaming on his favorite corner of the rug. Or, you may have to make the most painful of decisions: to end your Boxer's incurable suffering in the most humane way possible, via veterinary euthanasia.

Euthanasia is, simply, an overdose of anaesthesia. The dog will peacefully go to sleep before the overdose causes his heart to stop. If you make this difficult choice (and it is wrenching), steel yourself and remain with your dog while the procedure is being performed. Remember—your Boxer does not know what is happening, and the last thing you should want him to remember is the soothing sound of your voice as he drifts asleep. You owe him no less; it has been a remarkable journey.

Your Happy, Healthy Pet

Your Dog's Name _____

Name on Your Dog's Pedigree (if your dog has one) _____

_____

Where Your Dog Came From _____

_____

Your Dog's Birthday _____

Your Dog's Veterinarian

    Name   _____

    Address   _____

    Phone Number_____

    Emergency Number_____

Your Dog's Health

    Vaccines

        type _____ date given _____

        type _____ date given _____

        type _____ date given _____

        type _____ date given _____

    Heartworm

        date tested _____ type used_____ start date _____

Your Dog's License Number_____

Groomer's Name and Number _____

Dogsitter/Walker's Name and Number _____

Awards Your Dog Has Won

    Award _____ date earned _____

    Award _____ date earned _____

part three

Enjoying
your
Dog

chapter 8

Basic
Training

by Ian Dunbar, Ph.D., MRCVS

Training is the jewel in the crown—the most important aspect of doggy husbandry. There is no more important variable influencing dog behavior and temperament than the dog's education: A well-trained, well-behaved and good-natured puppydog is always a joy to live with, but an untrained and uncivilized dog can be a perpetual nightmare. Moreover, deny the dog an education and she will not have the opportunity to fulfill her own canine potential; neither will she have the ability to communicate effectively with her human companions.

Luckily, modern psychological training methods are easy, efficient, effective and, above all, considerably dog-friendly and user-friendly.

Doggy education is as simple as it is enjoyable. But before you can have a good time play-training with your new dog, you have to learn what to do and how to do it. There is no bigger variable influencing the success of dog training than the *owner's* experience and expertise. *Before you embark on the dog's education, you must first educate yourself.*

Basic Training for Owners

Ideally, basic owner training should begin well *before* you select your dog. Find out all you can about your chosen breed first, then master rudimentary training and handling skills. If you already have your puppy-dog, owner training is a dire emergency—the clock is ticking! Especially for puppies, the first few weeks at home are the most important and influential days in the dog's life. Indeed, the cause of most adolescent and adult problems may be traced back to the initial days the pup explores her new home. This is the time to establish the *status quo*—to teach the puppydog how you would like her to behave and so prevent otherwise quite predictable problems.

In addition to consulting breeders and breed books such as this one (which understandably have a positive breed bias), seek out as many pet owners with your breed as you can find. Good points are obvious. What you want to find out are the breed-specific *problems,* so you can nip them in the bud. In particular, you should talk to owners with *adolescent* dogs and make a list of all anticipated problems. Most important, *test drive* at least half a dozen adolescent and adult dogs of your breed yourself. An 8-week-old puppy is deceptively easy to handle, but she will acquire adult size, speed and strength in just four months, so you should learn now what to prepare for.

Puppy and pet dog training classes offer a convenient venue to locate pet owners and observe dogs in action. For a list of suitable trainers in your area, contact the Association of Pet Dog Trainers (see chapter 13). You may also begin your basic owner training by observing other owners in class. Watch as many classes and test drive as many dogs as possible. Select an upbeat, dog-friendly, people-friendly, fun-and-games, puppydog pet training class to learn the ropes. Also, watch training videos and read training books. You must find out what to do and how to do it *before* you have to do it.

Principles of Training

Most people think training comprises teaching the dog to do things such as sit, speak and roll over, but even a 4-week-old pup knows how to do these things already. Instead, the first step in training involves teaching the dog human words for each dog behavior and activity and for each aspect of the dog's environment. That way you, the owner, can more easily participate in the dog's domestic education by directing her to perform specific actions appropriately, that is, at the right time, in the right place and so on. Training opens communication channels, enabling an educated dog to at least understand her owner's requests.

In addition to teaching a dog *what* we want her to do, it is also necessary to teach her *why* she should do what we ask. Indeed, 95 percent of training revolves around motivating the dog *to want to do* what we want. Dogs often understand what their owners want; they just don't see the point of doing it—especially when the owner's repetitively boring and seemingly senseless instructions are totally at odds with much more pressing and exciting doggy distractions. It is not so much the dog that is being stubborn or dominant; rather, it is the owner who has failed to acknowledge the dog's needs and feelings and to approach training from the dog's point of view.

THE MEANING OF INSTRUCTIONS

The secret to successful training is learning how to use training lures to predict or prompt specific behaviors—to coax the dog to do what you want *when* you want. Any highly valued object (such as a treat or toy) may be used as a lure, which the dog will follow with her eyes and nose. Moving the lure in specific ways entices the dog to move her nose, head and entire body in specific ways. In fact, by learning the art of manipulating various lures, it is possible to teach the dog to assume virtually any body position and perform any action. Once you have control over the expression of the dog's behaviors and can elicit any body position or behavior at will, you can easily teach the dog to perform on request.

Teach your dog words for each activity she needs to know, like down.

Tell your dog what you want her to do, use a lure to entice her to respond correctly, then profusely praise and maybe reward her once she performs the desired action. For example, verbally request "Tina, sit!" while you move a squeaky toy upwards and backwards over the dog's muzzle (lure-movement and hand signal), smile knowingly as she looks up (to follow the lure) and sits down (as a result of canine anatomical engineering), then praise her to distraction ("Gooood Tina!"). Squeak the toy, offer a training treat and give your dog and yourself a pat on the back.

Being able to elicit desired responses over and over enables the owner to reward the dog over and over. Consequently, the dog begins to think training is fun. For example, the more the dog is rewarded for sitting, the more she enjoys sitting. Eventually the dog comes to realize that, whereas most sitting is appreciated, sitting immediately upon request usually prompts especially enthusiastic praise and a slew of high-level rewards. The dog begins to sit on cue much of the time, showing that she is starting to grasp the meaning of the owner's verbal request and hand signal.

WHY COMPLY?

Most dogs enjoy initial lure-reward training and are only too happy to comply with their owners' wishes. Unfortunately, repetitive drilling without appreciative feedback tends to diminish the dog's enthusiasm until she eventually fails to see the point of complying anymore. Moreover, as the dog approaches adolescence she becomes more easily distracted as she develops other interests. Lengthy sessions with repetitive exercises tend to bore and demotivate both parties. If it's not fun, the owner doesn't do it and neither does the dog.

Integrate training into your dog's life: The greater number of training sessions each day and the *shorter* they are, the more willingly compliant your dog will become. Make sure to have a short (just a few seconds) training interlude before every enjoyable canine activity. For example, ask your dog to sit to greet people, to sit before you throw her Frisbee and to sit for her supper. Really, sitting is no different from a canine "Please."

To train your dog, you need gentle hands, a loving heart and a good attitude.

Also, include numerous short training interludes during every enjoyable canine pastime, for example, when playing with the dog or when she is running in the park. In this fashion, doggy distractions may be effectively converted into rewards for training. Just as all games have rules, fun becomes training . . . and training becomes fun.

Eventually, rewards actually become unnecessary to continue motivating your dog. If trained with consideration and kindness, performing the desired behaviors will become self-rewarding and, in a sense, your dog will motivate herself. Just as it is not necessary to reward a human companion during an enjoyable walk in the park, or following a game of tennis, it is hardly necessary to reward our best friend—the dog—for walking by our side or while playing fetch. Human company during enjoyable activities is reward enough for most dogs.

Even though your dog has become self-motivating, it's still good to praise and pet her a lot and offer rewards once in a while, especially for a good job well done. And if for no other reason, praising and rewarding others is good for the human heart.

PUNISHMENT

Without a doubt, lure-reward training is by far the best way to teach: Entice your dog to do what you want and then reward her for doing so. Unfortunately, a human shortcoming is to take the good for granted and to moan and groan at the bad. Specifically, the dog's many good behaviors are ignored while the owner focuses on punishing the dog for making mistakes. In extreme cases, instruction is *limited* to punishing mistakes made by a trainee dog, child, employee or husband, even though it has been proven punishment training is notoriously inefficient and ineffective and is decidedly unfriendly and combative. It teaches the dog that training is a drag, almost as quickly as it teaches the dog to dislike her trainer. Why treat our best friends like our worst enemies?

Punishment training is also much more laborious and time consuming. Whereas it takes only a finite amount of time to teach a dog what to chew, for example, it takes much, much longer to punish the dog for each and every mistake. Remember, *there is only one right way!* So why not teach that right way from the outset?!

To make matters worse, punishment training causes severe lapses in the dog's reliability. Since it is obviously impossible to punish the dog each and every time she misbehaves, the dog quickly learns to distinguish between those times when she must comply (so as to avoid impending punishment) and those times when she need not comply, because punishment is impossible. Such times include when the dog is off leash and 6 feet away, when the owner is otherwise engaged (talking to a friend, watching television, taking a shower, tending to the baby or chatting on the telephone) or when the dog is left at home alone.

Instances of misbehavior will be numerous when the owner is away, because even when the dog complied in the owner's looming presence, she did so unwillingly. The dog was forced to act against her will, rather than molding her will to want to please. Hence, when the owner is absent, not only does the dog know she need not comply, she simply does not want to. Again, the trainee is not a stubborn vindictive beast, but rather the trainer has failed to teach. Punishment training invariably creates unpredictable Jekyll and Hyde behavior.

Trainer's Tools

Many training books extol the virtues of a vast array of training paraphernalia and electronic and metallic gizmos, most of which are designed for canine restraint, correction and punishment, rather than for actual facilitation of doggy education. In reality, most effective training tools are not found in stores; they come from within ourselves. In addition to a willing dog, all you really need is a functional human brain, gentle hands, a loving heart and a good attitude.

In terms of equipment, all dogs do require a quality buckle collar to sport dog tags and to attach the leash (for safety and to comply with local leash laws). Hollow chew toys (like Kongs or sterilized longbones) and a dog bed or collapsible crate are musts for housetraining. Three additional tools are required:

1. specific lures (training treats and toys) to predict and prompt specific desired behaviors;

2. rewards (praise, affection, training treats and toys) to reinforce for the dog what a lot of fun it all is; and

3. knowledge—how to convert the dog's favorite activities and games (potential distractions to training) into "life-rewards," which may be employed to facilitate training.

The most powerful of these is *knowledge.* Education is the key! Watch training classes, participate in training classes, watch videos, read books, enjoy play-training with your dog and then your dog will say "Please," and your dog will say "Thank you!"

Housetraining

If dogs were left to their own devices, certainly they would chew, dig and bark for entertainment and then no doubt highlight a few areas of their living space with sprinkles of urine, in much the same way we decorate by hanging pictures. Consequently, when we ask a dog to live with us, we must teach her *where* she may dig, *where* she may perform her toilet duties, *what* she may chew and *when* she may bark. After all, when left at home alone for many hours, we cannot expect the dog to amuse herself by completing crosswords or watching the soaps on TV!

Also, it would be decidedly unfair to keep the house rules a secret from the dog, and then get angry and punish the poor critter for inevitably transgressing rules she did not even know existed. Remember: Without adequate education and guidance, the dog will be forced to establish her own rules—doggy rules—and most probably will be at odds with the owner's view of domestic living.

Since most problems develop during the first few days the dog is at home, prospective dog owners must be certain they are quite clear about the principles of housetraining *before* they get a dog. Early misbehaviors quickly become established as the *status quo—*

becoming firmly entrenched as hard-to-break bad habits, which set the precedent for years to come. Make sure to teach your dog good habits right from the start. Good habits are just as hard to break as bad ones!

Ideally, when a new dog comes home, try to arrange for someone to be present as much as possible during the first few days (for adult dogs) or weeks for puppies. With only a little forethought, it is surprisingly easy to find a puppy sitter, such as a retired person, who would be willing to eat from your refrigerator and watch your television while keeping an eye on the newcomer to encourage the dog to play with chew toys and to ensure she goes outside on a regular basis.

POTTY TRAINING

To teach the dog where to relieve herself:

1. never let her make a single mistake;
2. let her know where you want her to go; and
3. handsomely reward her for doing so: "GOOOOOOOD DOG!!!" liver treat, liver treat, liver treat!

Preventing Mistakes

A single mistake is a training disaster, since it heralds many more in future weeks. And each time the dog soils the house, this further reinforces the dog's unfortunate preference for an indoor, carpeted toilet. *Do not let an unhousetrained dog have full run of the house.*

When you are away from home, or cannot pay full attention, confine the dog to an area where elimination is appropriate, such as an outdoor run or, better still, a small, comfortable indoor kennel with access to an outdoor run. When confined in this manner, most dogs will naturally housetrain themselves.

If that's not possible, confine the dog to an area, such as a utility room, kitchen, basement or garage, where elimination may not be desired in the long run but as an interim measure it is certainly preferable to doing it all around the house. Use newspaper to cover the floor of the dog's day room. The newspaper may be used to soak up the urine and to wrap up and dispose of the feces. Once your dog develops a preferred spot for eliminating, it is only necessary to cover that part of the floor with newspaper. The smaller papered area may then be moved (only a little each day) towards the door to the outside. Thus the dog will develop the tendency to go to the door when she needs to relieve herself.

Never confine an unhousetrained dog to a crate for long periods. Doing so would force the dog to soil the crate and ruin its usefulness as an aid for housetraining (see the following discussion).

Teaching Where

In order to teach your dog where you would like her to do her business, you have to be there to direct the proceedings—an obvious, yet often neglected, fact of life. In order to be there to teach the dog *where* to go, you need to know *when* she needs to go. Indeed, the success of housetraining depends on the owner's ability to predict these times. Certainly, a regular feeding schedule will facilitate prediction somewhat, but there is nothing like "loading the deck" and influencing the timing of the outcome yourself!

The first few weeks at home are the most important and influential in your dog's life.

Whenever you are at home, make sure the dog is under constant supervision and/or confined to a small area. If already well trained, simply instruct the dog to lie down in her bed or basket. Alternatively, confine the dog to a crate (doggy den) or tie-down (a short, 18-inch lead that can be clipped to an eye hook in the baseboard near her bed). Short-term close confinement strongly inhibits urination and defecation, since the dog does not want to soil her sleeping area. Thus, when you release the puppydog each hour, she will definitely need to urinate immediately and defecate every third or fourth hour. Keep the dog confined to her doggy den and take her to her intended toilet area each hour, every hour and on the hour.

When taking your dog outside, instruct her to sit quietly before opening the door—she will soon learn to sit by the door when she needs to go out!

Teaching Why

Being able to predict when the dog needs to go enables the owner to be on the spot to praise and reward the dog. Each hour, hurry the dog to the intended toilet area in the yard, issue the appropriate instruction ("Go pee!" or "Go poop!"), then give the dog three to four minutes to produce. Praise and offer a couple of training treats when successful. The treats are important because many people fail to praise their dogs with feeling . . . and housetraining is hardly the time for understatement. So either loosen up and enthusiastically praise that dog: "Wuzzzer-wuzzer-wuzzer, hoooser good wuffer den? Hoooo went pee for Daddy?" Or say "Good dog!" as best you can and offer the treats for effect.

Following elimination is an ideal time for a spot of play-training in the yard or house. Also, an empty dog may be allowed greater freedom around the house for the next half hour or so, just as long as you keep an eye out to make sure she does not get into other kinds of mischief. If you are preoccupied and cannot pay full attention, confine the dog to her doggy den once more to enjoy a peaceful snooze or to play with her many chew toys.

If your dog does not eliminate within the allotted time outside—no biggie! Back to her doggy den, and then try again after another hour.

As I own large dogs, I always feel more relaxed walking an empty dog, knowing that I will not need to finish our stroll weighted down with bags of feces!

Beware of falling into the trap of walking the dog to get her to eliminate. The good ol' dog walk is such an enormous highlight in the dog's life that it represents the single biggest potential reward in domestic dogdom. However, when in a hurry, or during inclement weather, many owners abruptly terminate the walk the moment the dog has done her business. This, in effect, severely punishes the dog for doing the right thing, in the right place at the right time. Consequently, many dogs become strongly inhibited from eliminating outdoors because they know it will signal an abrupt end to an otherwise thoroughly enjoyable walk.

Instead, instruct the dog to relieve herself in the yard prior to going for a walk. If you follow the above instructions, most dogs soon learn to eliminate on cue. As soon as the dog eliminates, praise (and offer a treat or two)—"Good dog! Let's go walkies!" Use the walk as a reward for eliminating in the yard. If the dog does not go, put her back in her doggy den and think about a walk later on. You will find with a "No feces—no walk" policy, your dog will become one of the fastest defecators in the business.

If you do not have a backyard, instruct the dog to eliminate right outside your front door prior to the walk. Not only will this facilitate clean up and disposal of the feces in your own trash can but, also, the walk may again be used as a colossal reward.

CHEWING AND BARKING

Short-term close confinement also teaches the dog that occasional quiet moments are a reality of domestic living. Your puppydog is extremely impressionable during her first few weeks at home. Regular confinement at this time soon exerts a calming influence over the dog's personality. Remember, once the dog is housetrained and calmer, there will be a whole lifetime ahead for the dog to enjoy full run of the house and garden. On the other hand, by letting the newcomer have unrestricted access to the entire household and allowing her to run willy-nilly, she will most certainly develop a bunch of behavior problems in short order, no doubt necessitating confinement later in life. It would not be fair to remedially restrain and confine a dog you have trained, through neglect, to run free.

When confining the dog, make sure she always has an impressive array of suitable chew toys. Kongs and sterilized longbones (both readily available from pet stores) make the best chew toys, since they are hollow and may be stuffed with treats to heighten the dog's interest. For example, by stuffing the little hole at the top of a Kong with a small piece of freeze-dried liver, the dog will not want to leave it alone.

Remember, treats do not have to be junk food and they certainly should not represent extra calories. Rather, treats should be part of each dog's regular

Make sure your puppy has suitable chew toys.

daily diet: Some food may be served in the dog's bowl for breakfast and dinner, some food may be used as training treats, and some food may be used for stuffing chew toys. I regularly stuff my dogs' many Kongs with different shaped biscuits and kibble. The kibble seems to fall out fairly easily, as do the oval-shaped biscuits, thus rewarding the dog instantaneously for checking out the chew toys. The bone-shaped biscuits fall out after a while, rewarding the dog for worrying at the chew toy. But the triangular biscuits never come out. They remain inside the Kong as lures, maintaining the dog's fascination with her chew toy. To further focus the dog's interest, I always make sure to flavor the triangular biscuits by rubbing them with a little cheese or freeze-dried liver.

If stuffed chew toys are reserved especially for times the dog is confined, the puppydog will soon learn to enjoy quiet moments in her doggy den and she will quickly develop a chew-toy habit— a good habit! This is a simple *autoshaping* process; all the owner has to do is set up the situation and the dog all but trains herself— easy and effective. Even when the dog is given run of the house, her first inclination will be to indulge her rewarding chew-toy habit rather than destroy less-attractive household articles, such as curtains, carpets, chairs and compact disks. Similarly, a chew-toy chewer will be less inclined to scratch and chew herself excessively. Also, if the dog busies herself as a recreational chewer, she will be less inclined to develop into a recreational barker or digger when left at home alone.

Stuff a number of chew toys whenever the dog is left confined and remove the extra-special-tasting treats when you return. Your dog will now amuse herself with her chew toys before falling asleep and then resume playing with her chew toys when she expects you to return. Since most owner-absent misbehavior happens right after you leave and right before your expected return, your puppydog will now be conveniently preoccupied with her chew toys at these times.

Come and Sit

Most puppies will happily approach virtually anyone, whether called or not; that is, until they collide with adolescence and

develop other more important doggy interests, such as sniffing a multiplicity of exquisite odors on the grass. Your mission, Mr./Ms. Owner, is to teach and reward the pup for coming reliably, willingly and happily when called—and you have just three months to get it done. Unless adequately reinforced, your puppy's tendency to approach people will self-destruct by adolescence.

Call your dog ("Tina, come!"), open your arms (and maybe squat down) as a welcoming signal, waggle a treat or toy as a lure and reward the puppydog when she comes running. Do not wait to praise the dog until she reaches you—she may come 95 percent of the way and then run off after some distraction. Instead, praise the dog's *first* step towards you and continue praising enthusiastically for *every* step she takes in your direction.

When the rapidly approaching puppy dog is three lengths away from impact, instruct her to sit ("Tina, sit!") and hold the lure in front of you in an outstretched hand to prevent her from hitting you mid-chest and knocking you flat on your back! As Tina decelerates to nose the lure, move the treat upwards and backwards just over her muzzle with an upwards motion of your extended arm (palm-upwards). As the dog looks up to follow the lure, she will sit down (if she jumps up, you are holding the lure too high). Praise the dog for sitting. Move backwards and call her again. Repeat this many times over, always praising when Tina comes and sits; on occasion, reward her.

For the first couple of trials, use a training treat both as a lure to entice the dog to come and sit and as a reward for doing so. Thereafter, try to use different items as lures and rewards. For example, lure the dog with a Kong or Frisbee but reward her with a food treat. Or lure the dog with a food treat but pat her and throw a tennis ball as a reward. After just a few repetitions, dispense with the lures and rewards; the dog will begin to respond willingly to your verbal requests and hand signals just for the prospect of praise from your heart and affection from your hands.

Instruct every family member, friend and visitor how to get the dog to come and sit. Invite people over for a series of pooch parties; do not keep the pup a secret— let other people enjoy this puppy, and let the pup enjoy other people. Puppydog parties are not only fun, they easily attract a lot of people to help *you* train *your* dog. Unless you teach your dog how to meet people, that is, to sit for greetings, no doubt the dog will resort to jumping up. Then you and the visitors will get annoyed, and the dog will be punished. This is not fair. *Send out those invitations for puppy parties and teach your dog to be mannerly and socially acceptable.*

Even though your dog quickly masters obedient recalls in the house, her reliability may falter when playing in the backyard or local park. Ironically, it is *the owner* who has unintentionally trained the dog *not* to respond in these instances. By allowing the dog to play and run around and otherwise have a good time, but then to call the dog to put her on leash to take her home, the dog quickly learns playing is fun but training is a drag. Thus, playing in the park becomes a severe distraction, which works against training. Bad news!

Instead, whether playing with the dog off leash or on leash, request her to come at frequent intervals—say, every minute or so. On most occasions, praise and pet the dog for a few seconds while she is sitting, then tell her to go play again. For especially fast recalls, offer a couple of training treats and take the time to praise and pet the dog enthusiastically before releasing her. The dog will learn that coming when called is not necessarily the end of the play session, and neither is it the end of the world; rather, it signals an enjoyable, quality time-out with the owner before resuming play once more. In fact, playing in the park now becomes a very effective life-reward, which works to facilitate training by reinforcing each obedient and timely recall. Good news!

Sit, Down, Stand and Rollover

Teaching the dog a variety of body positions is easy for owner and dog, impressive for spectators and extremely useful for all. Using lure-reward techniques, it is possible to train several positions at once to verbal commands or hand signals (which impress the socks off onlookers).

Sit and **down**—the two control commands—prevent or resolve nearly a hundred behavior problems. For example, if the dog happily and obediently sits or lies down when requested, she cannot jump on visitors, dash out the front door, run around and chase her tail, pester other dogs, harass cats or annoy family, friends or strangers. Additionally, "Sit" or "Down" are the best emergency commands for off-leash control.

It is easier to teach and maintain a reliable sit than maintain a reliable recall. *Sit* is the purest and simplest of commands—either the dog is sitting or she is not. If there is any change of circumstances or potential danger in the park, for example, simply instruct the dog to sit. If she sits, you have a number of options: Allow the dog to resume playing when she is safe, walk up and put the dog on leash or call the dog. The dog will be much more likely to come when called if she has already acknowledged her compliance by sitting. If the dog does not sit in the park—train her to!

Stand and *rollover-stay* are the two positions for examining the dog. Your veterinarian will love you to distraction if you take a little time to teach the dog to stand still and roll over and play possum. Also, your vet bills will be smaller because it will take the veterinarian less time to examine your dog. The rollover-stay is an especially useful command and is really just a variation of the down-stay: Whereas the dog lies prone in the traditional down, she lies supine in the rollover-stay.

As with teaching come and sit, the training techniques to teach the dog to assume all other body positions on cue are user-friendly and dog-friendly. Simply give the appropriate request, lure the dog into the desired body position using a training treat or toy and then *praise* (and maybe reward) the dog as soon as she complies. Try not to touch the dog to get her to respond. If you teach the dog by guiding her into position, the dog will quickly learn that rump-pressure means sit, for example, but as yet you still have no control over your dog if she is just 6 feet away. It will still be necessary to teach the dog to sit on request. So do not make training a time-consuming two-step process; instead, teach the dog to sit to a verbal request or hand signal from the outset. Once the dog sits willingly when requested, by all means use your hands to pet the dog when she does so.

To teach **down** when the dog is already sitting, say "Tina, down!," hold the lure in one hand (palm down) and lower that hand to the floor between the dog's forepaws. As the dog lowers her head to follow the lure, slowly move the lure away from the dog just a fraction (in front of her paws). The dog will lie down as she stretches her nose forward to follow the lure. Praise the dog when she does so. If the dog stands up, you pulled the lure away too far and too quickly.

When teaching the dog to lie down from the standing position, say "Down" and lower the lure to the floor as before. Once the dog has lowered her forequarters and assumed a play bow, gently and slowly move the lure *towards* the dog between her forelegs. Praise the dog as soon as her rear end plops down.

After just a couple of trials it will be possible to alternate sits and downs and have the dog energetically perform doggy push-ups. Praise the dog a lot, and after half a dozen or so push-ups reward the dog with a training treat or toy. You will notice the more energetically you move your arm—upwards (palm up) to get the dog to sit, and downwards (palm down) to get the dog to lie down—the more energetically the dog responds to your requests. Now try training the dog in silence and you will notice she has also learned to respond to hand signals. Yeah! Not too shabby for the first session.

To teach **stand** from the sitting position, say "Tina, stand," slowly move the lure half a dog-length away from the dog's nose, keeping it at nose level, and praise the dog as she stands to follow the lure. As soon

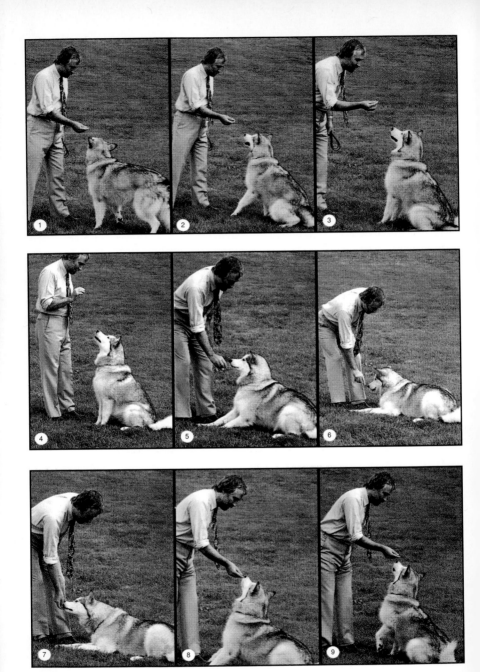

Using a food lure to teach sit, down and stand. 1) "Phoenix, sit." 2) Hand palm upwards, move lure up and back over dog's muzzle. 3) "Good sit, Phoenix!" 4) "Phoenix, down." 5) Hand palm downwards, move lure down to lie between dog's forepaws. 6) "Phoenix, off. Good down, Phoenix!" 7) "Phoenix, sit!" 8) Palm upwards, move lure up and back, keeping it close to dog's muzzle. 9) "Good sit, Phoenix!"

10) *"Phoenix, stand!"* 11) *Move lure away from dog at nose height, then lower it a tad.* 12) *"Phoenix, off! Good stand, Phoenix!"* 13) *"Phoenix, down!"* 14) *Hand palm downwards, move lure down to lie between dog's forepaws.* 15) *"Phoenix, off! Good down-stay, Phoenix!"* 16) *"Phoenix, stand!"* 17) *Move lure away from dog's muzzle up to nose height.* 18) *"Phoenix, off! Good stand-stay, Phoenix. Now we'll make the vet and groomer happy!"*

as the dog stands, lower the lure to just beneath the dog's chin to entice her to look down; otherwise she will stand and then sit immediately. To prompt the dog to stand from the down position, move the lure half a dog-length upwards and away from the dog, holding the lure at standing nose height from the floor.

Teaching *rollover* is best started from the down position, with the dog lying on one side, or at least with both hind legs stretched out on the same side. Say "Tina, bang!" and move the lure backwards and alongside the dog's muzzle to her elbow (on the side of her outstretched hind legs). Once the dog looks to the side and backwards, very slowly move the lure upwards to the dog's shoulder and backbone. Tickling the dog in the goolies (groin area) often invokes a reflex-raising of the hind leg as an appeasement gesture, which facilitates the tendency to roll over. If you move the lure too quickly and the dog jumps into the standing position, have patience and start again. As soon as the dog rolls onto her back, keep the lure stationary and mesmerize the dog with a relaxing tummy rub.

To teach *rollover-stay* when the dog is standing or moving, say "Tina, bang!" and give the appropriate hand signal (with index finger pointed and thumb cocked in true Sam Spade fashion), then in one fluid movement lure her to first lie down and then rollover-stay as above.

Teaching the dog to *stay* in each of the above four positions becomes a piece of cake after first teaching the dog not to worry at the toy or treat training lure. This is best accomplished by hand feeding dinner kibble. Hold a piece of kibble firmly in your hand and softly instruct "Off!" Ignore any licking and slobbering *for however long the dog worries at the treat*, but say "Take it!" and offer the kibble *the instant* the dog breaks contact with her muzzle. Repeat this a few times, and then up the ante and insist the dog remove her muzzle for one whole second before offering the kibble. Then progressively refine your criteria and have the dog not touch your hand (or treat) for longer and longer periods on each trial, such as for two seconds, four seconds, then six, ten, fifteen, twenty, thirty seconds and so on.

The dog soon learns: (1) worrying at the treat never gets results, whereas (2) noncontact is often rewarded after a variable time lapse.

Teaching *"Off!"* has many useful applications in its own right. Additionally, instructing the dog not to touch a training lure often produces spontaneous and magical stays. Request the dog to stand-stay, for example, and not to touch the lure. At first set your sights on a short two-second stay before rewarding the dog. (Remember, every long journey begins with a single step.) However, on subsequent trials, gradually and progressively increase the length of stay required to receive a reward. In no time at all your dog will stand calmly for a minute or so.

Relevancy Training

Once you have taught the dog what you expect her to do when requested to come, sit, lie down, stand, roll-over and stay, the time is right to teach the dog *why* she should comply with your wishes. The secret is to have many (*many*) extremely short training interludes (two to five seconds each) at numerous (*numerous*) times during the course of the dog's day. Especially work with the dog immediately *before* the dog's good times and *during* the dog's good times. For example, ask your dog to sit and/or lie down each time before opening doors, serving meals, offering treats and tummy rubs; ask the dog to perform a few controlled doggy push-ups before letting her off leash or throwing a tennis ball; and perhaps request the dog to sit-down-sit-stand-down-stand-rollover before inviting her to cuddle on the couch.

Similarly, request the dog to sit many times during play or on walks, and in no time at all the dog will be only too pleased to follow your instructions because she has learned that a compliant response heralds all sorts of goodies. Basically all you are trying to teach the dog is how to say please: "Please throw the tennis ball. Please may I snuggle on the couch."

Remember, it is important to keep training interludes short and to have many short sessions each and every day. The shortest (and most useful) session comprises asking the dog to sit and then go play during a play session. When trained this way, your dog will soon associate training with good times. In fact, the dog may be unable to distinguish between training and good times and, indeed, there should be no distinction. The warped concept that training involves forcing the dog to comply and/or dominating her will is totally at odds with the picture of a truly well-trained dog. In reality, enjoying a game of training with a dog is no different from enjoying a game of backgammon or tennis with a friend; and walking with a dog should be no different from strolling with a spouse, or with buddies on the golf course.

Walk by Your Side

Many people attempt to teach a dog to heel by putting her on a leash and physically correcting the dog when she makes mistakes. There are a number of things seriously wrong with this approach, the first being that most people do not want precision heeling; rather, they simply want the dog to follow or walk by their side. Second, when physically restrained during "training," even though the dog may grudgingly mope by your side when "handcuffed" on leash, let's see what happens when she is off leash. History! The dog is in the next county because she never enjoyed walking with you on leash and you have no control over her off leash. So let's just teach the dog off leash from the outset to *want* to walk with us. Third, if the dog has not been trained to heel, it is a trifle hasty to think about punishing the poor dog for making mistakes and breaking heeling rules she didn't even know existed. This is simply not fair! Surely, if the dog had been adequately taught how to heel, she would seldom make mistakes and hence there would be no need to correct the dog. Remember, each mistake and each correction (punishment) advertise the trainer's inadequacy, not the dog's. The dog is not stubborn, she is not stupid and she is not bad. Even if she were, she would still require training, so let's train her properly.

Let's teach the dog to *enjoy* following us and to *want* to walk by our side off leash. Then it will be easier to teach high-precision off-leash heeling patterns if desired. Before going on outdoor walks, it is necessary to teach the dog not to pull. Then it becomes easy to teach on-leash walking and heeling because the dog already wants to walk with you, she is familiar with the desired walking and heeling positions and she knows not to pull.

FOLLOWING

Start by training your dog to follow you. Many puppies will follow if you simply walk away from them and maybe click your fingers or chuckle. Adult dogs may require additional enticement to stimulate them to follow, such as a training lure or, at the very least, a lively trainer. To teach the dog to follow: (1) keep walking and (2) walk away from the dog. If the dog attempts to lead or lag, change pace; slow down if the dog forges too far ahead, but speed up if she lags too far behind. Say "Steady!" or "Easy!" each time before you slow down and "Quickly!" or "Hustle!" each time before you speed up, and the dog will learn to change pace on cue. If the dog lags or leads too far, or if she wanders right or left, simply walk quickly in the opposite direction and maybe even run away from the dog and hide.

Practicing is a lot of fun; you can set up a course in your home, yard or park to do this. Indoors, entice the dog to follow upstairs, into a bedroom, into the bathroom, downstairs, around the living room couch, zigzagging between dining room chairs and into the kitchen for dinner. Outdoors, get the dog to follow around park benches, trees, shrubs and along walkways and lines in the grass. (For safety outdoors, it is advisable to attach a long line on the dog, but never exert corrective tension on the line.)

Enjoying Your
Dog

Remember, following has a lot to do with attitude—
your attitude! Most probably your dog will *not* want to
follow Mr. Grumpy Troll with the personality of wilted
lettuce. Lighten up—walk with a jaunty step, whistle a
happy tune, sing, skip and tell jokes to your dog and
she will be right there by your side.

By Your Side

It is smart to train the dog to walk close on one side or
the other—either side will do, your choice. When walking, jogging or cycling, it is generally bad news to have
the dog suddenly cut in front of you. In fact, I train my
dogs to walk "By my side" and "Other side"—both very
useful instructions. It is possible to position the dog
fairly accurately by looking to the appropriate side and
clicking your fingers or slapping your thigh on that
side. A precise positioning may be attained by holding
a training lure, such as a chew toy, tennis ball or food
treat. Stop and stand still several times throughout the
walk, just as you would when window shopping or
meeting a friend. Use the lure to make sure the dog
slows down and stays close whenever you stop.

When teaching the dog to heel, we generally want
her to sit in heel position when we stop. Teach heel

*Using a toy to teach sit-heel-sit sequences: 1) "Phoenix, sit!" Standing still, move lure up and back over dog's
muzzle . . . 2) to position dog sitting in heel position on your left side. 3) Say "Phoenix, heel!" and walk ahead,
wagging lure in left hand. Change lure to right hand in preparation for sit signal. Say "Sit" and then . . .*

position at the standstill and the dog will learn that the default heel position is sitting by your side (left or right—your choice, unless you wish to compete in obedience trials, in which case the dog must heel on the left).

Several times a day, stand up and call your dog to come and sit in heel position—"Tina, heel!" For example, instruct the dog to come to heel each time there are commercials on TV, or each time you turn a page of a novel, and the dog will get it in a single evening.

Practice straight-line heeling and turns separately. With the dog sitting at heel, teach her to turn in place. After each quarter-turn, half-turn or full turn in place, lure the dog to sit at heel. Now it's time for short straight-line heeling sequences, no more than a few steps at a time. Always think of heeling in terms of sit-heel-sit sequences—start and end with the dog in position and do your best to keep her there when moving. Progressively increase the number of steps in each sequence. When the dog remains close for 20 yards of straight-line heeling, it is time to add a few turns and then sign up for a happy-heeling obedience class to get some advice from the experts.

4) use hand signal to lure dog to sit as you stop. Eventually, dog will sit automatically at heel whenever you stop. 5) "Good dog!"

No Pulling on Leash

You can start teaching your dog not to pull on leash anywhere—in front of the television or outdoors—but regardless of location, you must not take a single step with tension in the leash. For a reason known only to dogs, even just a couple of paces of pulling on leash is intrinsically motivating and diabolically rewarding. Instead, attach the leash to the dog's collar, grasp the other end firmly with both hands held close to your chest, and stand still—do not budge an inch. Have somebody watch you with a stopwatch to time your progress, or else you will never believe this will work and so you will not even try the exercise, and your shoulder and the dog's neck will be traumatized for years to come.

Stand still and wait for the dog to stop pulling, and to sit and/or lie down. All dogs stop pulling and sit eventually. Most take only a couple of minutes; the all-time record is 22½ minutes. Time how long it takes. Gently praise the dog when she stops pulling, and as soon as she sits, enthusiastically praise the dog and take just one step forward, then immediately stand still. This single step usually demonstrates the ballistic reinforcing nature of pulling on leash; most dogs explode to the end of the leash, so be prepared for the strain. Stand firm and wait for the dog to sit again. Repeat this half a dozen times and you will probably notice a progressive reduction in the force of the dog's one-step explosions and a radical reduction in the time it takes for the dog to sit each time.

As the dog learns "Sit we go" and "Pull we stop," she will begin to walk forward calmly with each single step and automatically sit when you stop. Now try two steps before you stop. Wooooooo! Scary! When the dog has mastered two steps at a time, try for three. After each success, progressively increase the number of steps in the sequence: try four steps and then six, eight, ten and twenty steps before stopping. Congratulations! You are now walking the dog on leash.

Whenever walking with the dog (off leash or on leash), make sure you stop periodically to practice a few position commands and stays before instructing the dog to "Walk on!" (Remember, you want the dog to be compliant everywhere, not just in the kitchen when her dinner is at hand.) For example, stopping every 25 yards to briefly train the dog amounts to over 200 training interludes within a single 3-mile stroll. And each training session is in a different location. You will not believe the improvement within just the first mile of the first walk.

To put it another way, integrating training into a walk offers 200 separate opportunities to use the continuance of the walk as a reward to reinforce the dog's education. Moreover, some training interludes may comprise continuing education for the dog's walking skills: Alternate short periods of the dog walking calmly by your side with periods when the dog is allowed to sniff and investigate the environment. Now sniffing odors on the grass and meeting other dogs become rewards which reinforce the dog's calm and mannerly demeanor. Good Lord! Whatever next? Many enjoyable walks together of course. Happy trails!

THE IMPORTANCE OF TRICKS

Nothing will improve a dog's quality of life better than having a few tricks under her belt. Teaching any trick expands the dog's vocabulary, which facilitates communication and improves the owner's control. Also, specific tricks help prevent and resolve specific behavior problems. For example, by teaching the dog to fetch her toys, the dog learns carrying a toy makes the owner happy and, therefore, will be more likely to chew her toy than other inappropriate items.

More important, teaching tricks prompts owners to lighten up and train with a sunny disposition. Really, tricks should be no different from any other behaviors we put on cue. But they are. When teaching tricks, owners have a much sweeter attitude, which in turn motivates the dog and improves her willingness to comply. The dog feels tricks are a blast, but formal commands are a drag. In fact, tricks are so enjoyable, they may be used as rewards in training by asking the dog to come, sit and down-stay and then rollover for a tummy rub. Go on, try it: Crack a smile and even giggle when the dog promptly and willingly lies down and stays.

Most important, performing tricks prompts onlookers to smile and giggle. Many people are scared of dogs, especially large ones. And nothing can be more off-putting for a dog than to be constantly confronted by strangers who don't like her because of her size or the way she looks. Uneasy people put the dog on edge, causing her to back off and bark, only frightening people all the more. And so a vicious circle develops, with the people's fear fueling the dog's fear *and vice versa*. Instead, tie a pink ribbon to your dog's collar and practice all sorts of tricks on walks and in the park, and you will be pleasantly amazed how it changes people's attitudes toward your friendly dog. The dog's repertoire of tricks is limited only by the trainer's imagination. Below I have described three of my favorites:

SPEAK AND SHUSH

The training sequence involved in teaching a dog to bark on request is no different from that used when training any behavior on cue: request—lure—response—reward. As always, the secret of success lies in finding an effective lure. If the dog always barks at the doorbell, for example, say "Rover, speak!", have an accomplice ring the doorbell, then reward the dog for barking. After a few woofs, ask Rover to "Shush!", waggle a food treat under her nose (to entice her to sniff and thus to shush), praise her when quiet and eventually offer the treat as a reward. Alternate "Speak" and "Shush," progressively increasing the length of shush-time between each barking bout.

PLAY BOW

With the dog standing, say "Bow!" and lower the food lure (palm upwards) to rest between the dog's forepaws. Praise as the dog lowers her forequarters and sternum to the ground (as when teaching the down), but then lure the dog to stand and offer the treat. On successive trials, gradually increase the length of time the dog is required to remain in the play bow posture in order to gain a food reward. If the dog's rear end collapses into a down, say nothing and offer no reward; simply start over.

BE A BEAR

With the dog sitting backed into a corner to prevent her from toppling over backwards, say "Be a bear!" With bent paw and palm down, raise a lure upwards and backwards along the top of the dog's muzzle. Praise the dog when she sits up on her haunches and offer the treat as a reward. To prevent the dog from standing on her hind legs, keep the lure closer to the dog's muzzle. On each trial, progressively increase the length of time the dog is required to sit up to receive a food reward. Since lure-reward training is so easy, teach the dog to stand and walk on her hind legs as well!

Teaching "Be a Bear"

chapter 9

Getting
Active
with your Dog

by Bardi McLennan

Once you and your dog have graduated from basic obedience training and are beginning to work together as a team, you can take part in the growing world of dog activities. There are so many fun things to do with your dog! Just remember, people and dogs don't always learn at the same pace, so don't be upset if you (or your dog) need more than two basic training courses before your team becomes operational. Even smart dogs don't go straight to college from kindergarten!

Just as there are events geared to certain types of dogs, so there are ones that are more appealing to certain types of people. In some

128

activities, you give the commands and your dog does the work (upland game hunting is one example), while in others, such as agility, you'll both get a workout. You may want to aim for prestigious titles to add to your dog's name, or you may want nothing more than the sheer enjoyment of being around other people and their dogs. Passive or active, participation has its own rewards.

Consider your dog's physical capabilities when looking into any of the canine activities. It's easy to see that a Basset Hound is not built for the racetrack, nor would a Chihuahua be the breed of choice for pulling a sled. A loyal dog will attempt almost anything you ask him to do, so it is up to you to know your dog's limitations. A dog must be physically sound in order to compete at any level in athletic activities, and being mentally sound is a definite plus. Advanced age, however, may not be a deterrent. Many dogs still hunt and herd at ten or twelve years of age. It's entirely possible for dogs to be "fit at 50." Take your dog for a checkup, explain to your vet the type of activity you have in mind and be guided by his or her findings.

All dogs seem to love playing flyball.

You needn't be restricted to breed-specific sports if it's only fun you're after. Certain AKC activities are limited to designated breeds; however, as each new trial, test or sport has grown in popularity, so has the variety of breeds encouraged to participate at a fun level.

But don't shortchange your fun, or that of your dog, by thinking only of the basic function of her breed. Once a dog has learned how to learn, she can be taught to do just about anything as long as the size of the dog is right for the job and you both think it is fun and rewarding. In other words, you are a team.

To get involved in any of the activities detailed in this chapter, look for the names and addresses of the organizations that sponsor them in Chapter 13. You can also ask your breeder or a local dog trainer for contacts.

You can compete in obedience trials with a well trained dog.

Official American Kennel Club Activities

The following tests and trials are some of the events sanctioned by the AKC and sponsored by various dog clubs. Your dog's expertise will be rewarded with impressive titles. You can participate just for fun, or be competitive and go for those awards.

OBEDIENCE

Training classes begin with pups as young as three months of age in kindergarten puppy training, then advance to pre-novice (all exercises on lead) and go on to novice, which is where you'll start off-lead work. In obedience classes dogs learn to sit, stay, heel and come through a variety of exercises. Once you've got the basics down, you can enter obedience trials and work toward earning your dog's first degree, a C.D. (Companion Dog).

The next level is called "Open," in which jumps and retrieves perk up the dog's interest. Passing grades in competition at this level earn a C.D.X. (Companion Dog Excellent). Beyond that lies the goal of the most ambitious—Utility (U.D. and even U.D.X. or OTCh, an Obedience Champion).

AGILITY

All dogs can participate in the latest canine sport to
have gained worldwide popularity for its fun and

excitement, agility. It began in England as a canine version of horse show-jumping, but because dogs are more agile and able to perform on verbal commands, extra feats were added such as climbing, balancing and racing through tunnels or in and out of weave poles. Many of the obstacles (regulation or homemade) can be set up in your own backyard. If the agility bug bites, you could end up in international competition!

For starters, your dog should be obedience trained, even though, in the beginning, the lessons may all be taught on lead. Once the dog understands the commands (and you do, too), it's as easy as guiding the dog over a prescribed course, one obstacle at a time. In competition, the race is against the clock, so wear your running shoes! The dog starts with 200 points and the judge deducts for infractions and misadventures along the way.

All dogs seem to love agility and respond to it as if they were being turned loose in a playground paradise. Your dog's enthusiasm will be contagious; agility turns into great fun for dog and owner.

FIELD TRIALS AND HUNTING TESTS

There are field trials and hunting tests for the sporting breeds—retrievers, spaniels and pointing breeds, and for some hounds—Bassets, Beagles and Dachshunds. Field trials are competitive events that test a dog's ability to perform the functions for which she was bred. Hunting tests, which are open to retrievers,

---

TITLES AWARDED BY THE AKC

Conformation: Ch. (Champion)

Obedience: CD (Companion Dog); CDX (Companion Dog Excellent); UD (Utility Dog); UDX (Utility Dog Excellent); OTCh. (Obedience Trial Champion)

Field: JH (Junior Hunter); SH (Senior Hunter); MH (Master Hunter); AFCh. (Amateur Field Champion); FCh. (Field Champion)

Lure Coursing: JC (Junior Courser); SC (Senior Courser)

Herding: HT (Herding Tested); PT (Pre-Trial Tested); HS (Herding Started); HI (Herding Intermediate); HX (Herding Excellent); HCh. (Herding Champion)

Tracking: TD (Tracking Dog); TDX (Tracking Dog Excellent)

Agility: NAD (Novice Agility); OAD (Open Agility); ADX (Agility Excellent); MAX (Master Agility)

Earthdog Tests: JE (Junior Earthdog); SE (Senior Earthdog); ME (Master Earthdog)

Canine Good Citizen: CGC

Combination: DC (Dual Champion—Ch. and Fch.); TC (Triple Champion—Ch., Fch., and OTCh.)

spaniels and pointing breeds only, are noncompetitive and are a means of judging the dog's ability as well as that of the handler.

Hunting is a very large and complex part of canine sports, and if you own one of the breeds that hunts, the events are a great treat for your dog and you. He gets to do what he was bred for, and you get to work with him and watch him do it. You'll be proud of and amazed at what your dog can do.

Fortunately, the AKC publishes a series of booklets on these events, which outline the rules and regulations and include a glossary of the sometimes complicated terms. The AKC also publishes newsletters for field trialers and hunting test enthusiasts. The United Kennel Club (UKC) also has informative materials for the hunter and his dog.

Retrievers and other sporting breeds get to do what they're bred to in hunting tests.

HERDING TESTS AND TRIALS

Herding, like hunting, dates back to the first known uses man made of dogs. The interest in herding today is widespread, and if you own a herding breed, you can join in the activity. Herding dogs are tested for their natural skills to keep a flock of ducks, sheep or cattle together. If your dog shows potential, you can start at the testing level, where your dog can earn a title for showing an inherent herding ability. With training you can advance to the trial level, where your dog should be capable of controlling even difficult livestock in diverse situations.

LURE COURSING

The AKC Tests and Trials for Lure Coursing are open to traditional sighthounds—Greyhounds, Whippets,

Borzoi, Salukis, Afghan Hounds, Ibizan Hounds and Scottish Deerhounds—as well as to Basenjis and Rhodesian Ridgebacks. Hounds are judged on overall ability, follow, speed, agility and endurance. This is possibly the most exciting of the trials for spectators, because the speed and agility of the dogs is awesome to watch as they chase the lure (or "course") in heats of two or three dogs at a time.

TRACKING

Tracking is another activity in which almost any dog can compete because every dog that sniffs the ground when taken outdoors is, in fact, tracking. The hard part comes when the rules as to what, when and where the dog tracks are determined by a person, not the dog! Tracking tests cover a large area of fields, woods and roads. The tracks are laid hours before the dogs go to work on them, and include "tricks" like cross-tracks and sharp turns. If you're interested in search-and-rescue work, this is the place to start.

This tracking dog is hot on the trail.

EARTHDOG TESTS FOR SMALL TERRIERS AND DACHSHUNDS

These tests are open to Australian, Bedlington, Border, Cairn, Dandie Dinmont, Smooth and Wire Fox, Lakeland, Norfolk, Norwich, Scottish, Sealyham, Skye, Welsh and West Highland White Terriers as well as Dachshunds. The dogs need no prior training for this terrier sport. There is a qualifying test on the day of the event, so dog and handler learn the rules on the spot. These tests, or "digs," sometimes end with informal races in the late afternoon.

133

Here are some of the extracurricular obedience and racing activities that are not regulated by the AKC or UKC, but are generally run by clubs or a group of dog fanciers and are often open to all.

Canine Freestyle This activity is something new on the scene and is variously likened to dancing, dressage or ice skating. It is meant to show the athleticism of the dog, but also requires showmanship on the part of the dog's handler. If you and your dog like to ham it up for friends, you might want to look into freestyle.

Lure coursing lets sighthounds do what they do best—run!

Scent Hurdle Racing Scent hurdle racing is purely a fun activity sponsored by obedience clubs with members forming competing teams. The height of the hurdles is based on the size of the shortest dog on the team. On a signal, one team dog is released on each of two side-by-side courses and must clear every hurdle before picking up its own dumbbell from a platform and returning over the jumps to the handler. As each dog returns, the next on that team is sent. Of course, that is what the dogs are supposed to do. When the dogs improvise (going under or around the hurdles, stealing another dog's dumbbell, and so forth), it no doubt frustrates the handlers, but just adds to the fun for everyone else.

Flyball This type of racing is similar, but after negotiating the four hurdles, the dog comes to a flyball box, steps on a lever that releases a tennis ball into the air, catches the ball and returns over the hurdles to the starting point. This game also becomes extremely fun for spectators because the dogs sometimes cheat by catching a ball released by the dog in the next lane. Three titles can be earned—Flyball Dog (F.D.), Flyball Dog Excellent (F.D.X.) and Flyball Dog Champion (Fb.D.Ch.)—all awarded by the North American Flyball Association, Inc.

Dogsledding The name conjures up the Rocky Mountains or the frigid North, but you can find dogsled clubs in such unlikely spots as Maryland, North Carolina and Virginia! Dogsledding is primarily for the Nordic breeds such as the Alaskan Malamutes, Siberian Huskies and Samoyeds, but other breeds can try. There are some practical backyard applications to this sport, too. With parental supervision, almost any strong dog could pull a child's sled.

Coming over the A-frame on an agility course.

These are just some of the many recreational ways you can get to know and understand your multifaceted dog better and have fun doing it.

chapter 10

Your Dog
and your
Family

by Bardi McLennan

Adding a dog automatically increases your family by one, no matter whether you live alone in an apartment or are part of a mother, father and six kids household. The single-person family is fair game for numerous and varied canine misconceptions as to who is dog and who pays the bills, whereas a dog in a houseful of children will consider himself to be just one of the gang, littermates all. One dog and one child may give a dog reason to believe they are both kids or both dogs.

Either interpretation requires parental supervision and sometimes speedy intervention.

As soon as one paw goes through the door into your home, Rufus (or Rufina) has to make many adjustments to become a part of your family. Your job is to make him fit in as painlessly as possible. An older dog may have some frame of reference from past experience, but to a 10-week-old puppy, everything is brand new: people, furniture, stairs, when and where people eat, sleep or watch TV, his own place and everyone else's space, smells, sounds, outdoors—everything!

Puppies, and newly acquired dogs of any age, do not need what we think of as "freedom." If you leave a new dog or puppy loose in the house, you will almost certainly return to chaotic destruction and the dog will forever after equate your homecoming with a time of punishment to be dreaded. It is unfair to give your dog what amounts to "freedom to get into trouble." Instead, confine him to a crate for brief periods of your absence (up to three or four hours) and, for the long haul, a workday for example, confine him to one untrashable area with his own toys, a bowl of water and a radio left on (low) in another room.

Lots of pets get along with each other just fine.

For the first few days, when not confined, put Rufus on a long leash tied to your wrist or waist. This umbilical cord method enables the dog to learn all about you from your body language and voice, and to learn by his own actions which things in the house are NO! and which ones are rewarded by "Good dog." Housetraining will be easier with the pup always by your side. Speaking of which, accidents do happen. That goal of "completely housetrained" takes up to a year, or the length of time it takes the pup to mature.

The All-Adult Family

Most dogs in an adults-only household today are likely to be latchkey pets, with no one home all day but the dog. When you return after a tough day on the job, the dog can and should be your relaxation therapy. But going home can instead be a daily frustration.

Separation anxiety is a very common problem for the dog in a working household. It may begin with whines and barks of loneliness, but it will soon escalate into a frenzied destruction derby. That is why it is so important to set aside the time to teach a dog to relax when left alone in his confined area and to understand that he can trust you to return.

Let the dog get used to your work schedule in easy stages. Confine him to one room and go in and out of that room over and over again. Be casual about it. No physical, voice or eye contact. When the pup no longer even notices your comings and goings, leave the house for varying lengths of time, returning to stay home for a few minutes and gradually increasing the time away. This training can take days, but the dog is learning that you haven't left him forever and that he can trust you.

Any time you leave the dog, but especially during this training period, be casual about your departure. No anxiety-building fond farewells. Just "Bye" and go! Remember the "Good dog" when you return to find everything more or less as you left it.

If things are a mess (or even a disaster) when you return, greet the dog, take him outside to eliminate, and then put him in his crate while you clean up. Rant and rave in the shower! *Do not* punish the dog. You were not there when it happened, and the rule is: Only punish as you catch the dog in the act of wrongdoing. Obviously, it makes sense to get your latchkey puppy when you'll have a week or two to spend on these training essentials.

Family weekend activities should include Rufus whenever possible. Depending on the pup's age, now is the time for a long walk in the park, playtime in the backyard, a hike in the woods. Socializing is as important as health care, good food and physical exercise, so visiting Aunt Emma or Uncle Harry and the next-door neighbor's dog or cat is essential to developing an outgoing, friendly temperament in your pet.

If you are a single adult, socializing Rufus at home and away will prevent him from becoming overly protective of you (or just overly attached) and will also prevent such behavioral problems as dominance or fear of strangers.

Babies

Whether already here or on the way, babies figure larger than life in the eyes of a dog. If the dog is there first, let him in on all your baby preparations in the house. When baby arrives, let Rufus sniff any item of clothing that has been on the baby before Junior comes home. Then let Mom greet the dog first before introducing the new family member. Hold the baby down for the dog to see and sniff, but make sure someone's holding the dog on lead in case of any sudden moves. Don't play keep-away or tease the dog with the baby, which only invites undesirable jumping up.

The dog and the baby are "family," and for starters can be treated almost as equals. Things rapidly change, however, especially when baby takes to creeping around on all fours on the dog's turf or, better yet, has yummy pudding all over her face and hands! That's when a lot of things in the dog's and baby's lives become more separate than equal.

Dogs are perfect confidants.

Toddlers make terrible dog owners, but if you can't avoid the combination, use patient discipline (that is, positive teaching rather than punishment), and use time-outs before you run out of patience.

A dog and a baby (or toddler, or an assertive young child) should never be left alone together. Take the dog with you or confine him. With a baby or youngsters in the house, you'll have plenty of use for that wonderful canine safety device called a crate!

Young Children

Any dog in a house with kids will behave pretty much as the kids do, good or bad. But even good dogs and good children can get into trouble when play becomes rowdy and active.

Teach children how to play nicely with a puppy.

Legs bobbing up and down, shrill voices screeching, a ball hurtling overhead, all add up to exuberant frustration for a dog who's just trying to be part of the gang. In a pack of puppies, any legs or toys being chased would be caught by a set of teeth, and all the pups involved would understand that is how the game is played. Kids do not understand this, nor do parents tolerate it. Bring Rufus indoors before you have reason to regret it. This is time-out, not a punishment.

You can explain the situation to the children and tell them they must play quieter games until the puppy learns not to grab them with his mouth. Unfortunately, you can't explain it that easily to the dog. With adult supervision, they will learn how to play together.

Young children love to tease. Sticking their faces or wiggling their hands or fingers in the dog's face is teasing. To another person it might be just annoying, but it is threatening to a dog. There's another difference: We can make the child stop by an explanation, but the only way a dog can stop it is with a warning growl and then with teeth. Teasing is the major cause of children being bitten by their pets. Treat it seriously.

140

Older Children

The best age for a child to get a first dog is between the ages of 8 and 12. That's when kids are able to accept some real responsibility for their pet. Even so, take the child's vow of "I will never *ever* forget to feed (brush, walk, etc.) the dog" for what it's worth: a child's good intention at that moment. Most kids today have extra lessons, soccer practice, Little League, ballet, and so forth piled on top of school schedules. There will be many times when Mom will have to come to the dog's rescue. "I walked the dog for you so you can set the table for me" is one way to get around a missed appointment without laying on blame or guilt.

Kids in this age group make excellent obedience trainers because they are into the teaching/learning process themselves and they lack the self-consciousness of adults. Attending a dog show is something the whole family can enjoy, and watching Junior Showmanship may catch the eye of the kids. Older children can begin to get involved in many of the recreational activities that were reviewed in the previous chapter. Some of the agility obstacles, for example, can be set up in the backyard as a family project (with an adult making sure all the equipment is safe and secure for the dog).

Older kids are also beginning to look to the future, and may envision themselves as veterinarians or trainers or show dog handlers or writers of the next Lassie best-seller. Dogs are perfect confidants for these dreams. They won't tell a soul.

Other Pets

Introduce all pets tactfully. In a dog/cat situation, hold the dog, not the cat. Let two dogs meet on neutral turf—a stroll in the park or a walk down the street—with both on loose leads to permit all the normal canine ways of saying hello, including routine sniffing, circling, more sniffing, and so on. Small creatures such as hamsters, chinchillas or mice must be kept safe from their natural predators (dogs and cats).

Festive Family Occasions

Parties are great for people, but not necessarily for puppies. Until all the guests have arrived, put the dog in his crate or in a room where he won't be disturbed. A socialized dog can join the fun later as long as he's not underfoot, annoying guests or into the hors d'oeuvres.

There are a few dangers to consider, too. Doors opening and closing can allow a puppy to slip out unnoticed in the confusion, and you'll be organizing a search party instead of playing host or hostess. Party food and buffet service are not for dogs. Let Rufus party in his crate with a nice big dog biscuit.

At Christmas time, not only are tree decorations dangerous and breakable (and perhaps family heirlooms), but extreme caution should be taken with the lights, cords and outlets for the tree lights and any other festive lighting. Occasionally a dog lifts a leg, ignoring the fact that the tree is indoors. To avoid this, use a canine repellent, made for gardens, on the tree. Or keep him out of the tree room unless supervised. And whatever you do, *don't* invite trouble by hanging his toys on the tree!

Car Travel

Before you plan a vacation by car or RV with Rufus, be sure he enjoys car travel. Nothing spoils a holiday quicker than a carsick dog! Work within the dog's comfort level. Get in the car with the dog in his crate or attached to a canine car safety belt and just sit there until he relaxes. That's all. Next time, get in the car, turn on the engine and go nowhere. Just sit. When that is okay, turn on the engine and go around the block. Now you can go for a ride and include a stop where you get out, leaving the dog for a minute or two.

On a warm day, always park in the shade and leave windows open several inches. And return quickly. It only takes 10 minutes for a car to become an overheated steel death trap.

Motel or Pet Motel?

Not all motels or hotels accept pets, but you have a much better choice today than even a few years ago. To find a dog-friendly lodging, look at *On the Road Again With Man's Best Friend,* a series of directories that detail bed and breakfasts, inns, family resorts and other hotels/motels. Some places require a refundable deposit to cover any damage incurred by the dog. More B&Bs accept pets now, but some restrict the size.

If taking Rufus with you is not feasible, check out boarding kennels in your area. Your veterinarian may offer this service, or recommend a kennel or two he or she is familiar with. Go see the facilities for yourself, ask about exercise, diet, housing, and so on. Or, if you'd rather have Rufus stay home, look into bonded petsltters, many of whom will also bring in the mail and water your plants.

chapter 11

Your Dog
and your
Community

by Bardi McLennan

Step outside your home with your dog and you are no longer just family, you are both part of your community. This is when the phrase "responsible pet ownership" takes on serious implications. For starters, it means you pick up after your dog—not just occasionally, but every time your dog eliminates away from home. That means you have joined the Plastic Baggy Brigade! You always have plastic sandwich bags in your pocket and several in the car. It means you teach your kids how to use them, too. If you think this is "yucky," just imagine what the person (a non-doggy person) who inadvertently steps in the mess thinks!

Your responsibility extends to your neighbors: To their ears (no annoying barking); to their property (their garbage, their lawn, their flower beds, their cat—especially their cat); to their kids (on bikes, at play); to their kids' toys and sports equipment.

There are numerous dog-related laws, ranging from simple dog licensing and leash laws to those holding you liable for any physical injury or property damage done by your dog. These laws are in place to protect everyone in the community, including you and your dog. There are town ordinances and state laws which are by no means the same in all towns or all states. Ignorance of the law won't get you off the hook. The time to find out what the laws are where you live is now.

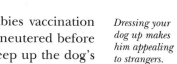

Be sure your dog's license is current. This is not just a good local ordinance, it can make the difference between finding your lost dog or not. Many states now require proof of rabies vaccination and that the dog has been spayed or neutered before issuing a license. At the same time, keep up the dog's annual immunizations.

Dressing your dog up makes him appealing to strangers.

Never let your dog run loose in the neighborhood. This will not only keep you on the right side of the leash law, it's the outdoor version of the rule about not giving your dog "freedom to get into trouble."

Good Canine Citizen

Sometimes it's hard for a dog's owner to assess whether or not the dog is sufficiently socialized to be accepted by the community at large. Does Rufus or Rufina display good, controlled behavior in public? The AKC's Canine Good Citizen program is available through many dog organizations. If your dog passes the test, the title "CGC" is earned.

The overall purpose is to turn your dog into a good neighbor and to teach you about your responsibility to your community as a dog owner. Here are the ten things your dog must do willingly:

1. Accept a stranger stopping to chat with you.
2. Sit and be petted by a stranger.
3. Allow a stranger to handle him or her as a groomer or veterinarian would.
4. Walk nicely on a loose lead.
5. Walk calmly through a crowd.
6. Sit and down on command, then stay in a sit or down position while you walk away.
7. Come when called.
8. Casually greet another dog.
9. React confidently to distractions.
10. Accept being left alone with someone other than you and not become overly agitated or nervous.

Schools and Dogs

Schools are getting involved with pet ownership on an educational level. It has been proven that children who are kind to animals are humane in their attitude toward other people as adults.

A dog is a child's best friend, and so children are often primary pet owners, if not the primary caregivers. Unfortunately, they are also the ones most often bitten by dogs. This occurs due to a lack of understanding that pets, no matter how sweet, cuddly and loving, are still animals. Schools, along with parents, dog clubs, dog fanciers and the AKC, are working to change all that with video programs for children not only in grade school, but in the nursery school and pre-kindergarten age group. Teaching youngsters how to be responsible dog owners is important community work. When your dog has a CGC, volunteer to take part in an educational classroom event put on by your dog club.

Boy Scout Merit Badge

A Merit Badge for Dog Care can be earned by any Boy Scout ages 11 to 18. The requirements are not easy, but amount to a complete course in responsible dog care and general ownership. Here are just a few of the things a Scout must do to earn that badge:

Point out ten parts of the dog using the correct names.

Give a report (signed by parent or guardian) on your care of the dog (feeding, food used, housing, exercising, grooming and bathing), plus what has been done to keep the dog healthy.

Explain the right way to obedience train a dog, and demonstrate three comments.

Several of the requirements have to do with health care, including first aid, handling a hurt dog, and the dangers of home treatment for a serious ailment.

The final requirement is to know the local laws and ordinances involving dogs.

There are similar programs for Girl Scouts and 4-H members.

Local Clubs

Local dog clubs are no longer in existence just to put on a yearly dog show. Today, they are apt to be the hub of the community's involvement with pets. Dog clubs conduct educational forums with big-name speakers, stage demonstrations of canine talent in a busy mall and take dogs of various breeds to schools for classroom discussion.

The quickest way to feel accepted as a member in a club is to volunteer your services! Offer to help with something—anything—and watch your popularity (and your interest) grow.

Therapy Dogs

Once your dog has earned that essential CGC and reliably demonstrates a steady, calm temperament, you could look into what therapy dogs are doing in your area.

Therapy dogs go with their owners to visit patients at hospitals or nursing homes, generally remaining on leash but able to coax a pat from a stiffened hand, a smile from a blank face, a few words from sealed lips or a hug from someone in need of love.

Nursing homes cover a wide range of patient care. Some specialize in care of the elderly, some in the treatment of specific illnesses, some in physical therapy. Children's facilities also welcome visits from trained therapy dogs for boosting morale in their pediatric patients. Hospice care for the terminally ill and the at-home care of AIDS patients are other areas where this canine visiting is desperately needed. Therapy dog training comes first.

Your dog can make a difference in lots of lives.

There is a lot more involved than just taking your nice friendly pooch to someone's bedside. Doing therapy dog work involves your own emotional stability as well as that of your dog. But once you have met all the requirements for this work, making the rounds once a week or once a month with your therapy dog is possibly the most rewarding of all community activities.

Disaster Aid

This community service is definitely not for everyone, partly because it is time-consuming. The initial training is rigorous, and there can be no let-up in the continuing workouts, because members are on call 24 hours a day to go wherever they are needed at a moment's notice. But if you think you would like to be able to assist in a disaster, look into search-and-rescue work. The network of search-and-rescue volunteers is worldwide, and all members of the American Rescue Dog Association (ARDA) who are qualified to do this work are volunteers who train and maintain their own dogs.

Physical Aid

Most people are familiar with Seeing Eye dogs, which serve as blind people's eyes, but not with all the other work that dogs are trained to do to assist the disabled. Dogs are also specially trained to pull wheelchairs, carry school books, pick up dropped objects, open and close doors. Some also are ears for the deaf. All these assistance-trained dogs, by the way, are allowed anywhere "No Pet" signs exist (as are therapy dogs when

Making the rounds with your therapy dog can be very rewarding.

properly identified). Getting started in any of this fascinating work requires a background in dog training and canine behavior, but there are also volunteer jobs ranging from answering the phone to cleaning out kennels to providing a foster home for a puppy. You have only to ask.

part four

Beyond
the
Basics

chapter 12

Recommended Reading

Books

ABOUT HEALTH CARE

Ackerman, Lowell. *Guide to Skin and Haircoat Problems in Dogs*. Loveland, Colo.: Alpine Publications, 1994.

Alderton, David. *The Dog Care Manual*. Hauppauge, N.Y.: Barron's Educational Series, Inc., 1986.

American Kennel Club. *American Kennel Club Dog Care and Training*. New York: Howell Book House, 1991.

Bamberger, Michelle, DVM. *Help! The Quick Guide to First Aid for Your Dog*. New York: Howell Book House, 1995.

Carlson, Delbert, DVM, and James Giffin, MD. *Dog Owner's Home Veterinary Handbook*. New York: Howell Book House, 1992.

DeBitetto, James, DVM, and Sarah Hodgson. *You & Your Puppy*. New York: Howell Book House, 1995.

Humphries, Jim, DVM. *Dr. Jim's Animal Clinic for Dogs*. New York: Howell Book House, 1994.

McGinnis, Terri. *The Well Dog Book*. New York: Random House, 1991.

Pitcairn, Richard and Susan. *Natural Health for Dogs*. Emmaus, Pa.: Rodale Press, 1982.

ABOUT DOG SHOWS

Hall, Lynn. *Dog Showing for Beginners*. New York: Howell Book House, 1994.

Nichols, Virginia Tuck. *How to Show Your Own Dog*. Neptune, N. J.: TFH, 1970.

Vanacore, Connie. *Dog Showing, An Owner's Guide*. New York: Howell Book House, 1990.

ABOUT TRAINING

Ammen, Amy. *Training in No Time.* New York: Howell Book House, 1995.

Baer, Ted. *Communicating With Your Dog.* Hauppauge, N.Y.: Barron's Educational Series, Inc., 1989.

Benjamin, Carol Lea. *Dog Problems.* New York: Howell Book House, 1989.

Benjamin, Carol Lea. *Dog Training for Kids.* New York: Howell Book House, 1988.

Benjamin, Carol Lea. *Mother Knows Best.* New York: Howell Book House, 1985.

Benjamin, Carol Lea. *Surviving Your Dog's Adolescence.* New York: Howell Book House, 1993.

Bohnenkamp, Gwen. *Manners for the Modern Dog.* San Francisco: Perfect Paws, 1990.

Dibra, Bashkim. *Dog Training by Bash.* New York: Dell, 1992.

Dunbar, Ian, PhD, MRCVS. *Dr. Dunbar's Good Little Dog Book,* James & Kenneth Publishers, 2140 Shattuck Ave. #2406, Berkeley, Calif. 94704. (510) 658–8588. Order from the publisher.

Dunbar, Ian, PhD, MRCVS. *How to Teach a New Dog Old Tricks,* James & Kenneth Publishers. Order from the publisher; address above.

Dunbar, Ian, PhD, MRCVS, and Gwen Bohnenkamp. Booklets on *Preventing Aggression; Housetraining; Chewing; Digging; Barking; Socialization; Fearfulness; and Fighting,* James & Kenneth Publishers. Order from the publisher; address above.

Evans, Job Michael. *People, Pooches and Problems.* New York: Howell Book House, 1991.

Kilcommons, Brian and Sarah Wilson. *Good Owners, Great Dogs.* New York: Warner Books, 1992.

McMains, Joel M. *Dog Logic—Companion Obedience.* New York: Howell Book House, 1992.

Rutherford, Clarice and David H. Neil, MRCVS. *How to Raise a Puppy You Can Live With.* Loveland, Colo.: Alpine Publications, 1982.

Volhard, Jack and Melissa Bartlett. *What All Good Dogs Should Know: The Sensible Way to Train.* New York: Howell Book House, 1991.

ABOUT BREEDING

Harris, Beth J. Finder. *Breeding a Litter, The Complete Book of Prenatal and Postnatal Care.* New York: Howell Book House, 1983.

Holst, Phyllis, DVM. *Canine Reproduction.* Loveland, Colo.: Alpine Publications, 1985.

Walkowicz, Chris and Bonnie Wilcox, DVM. *Successful Dog Breeding, The Complete Handbook of Canine Midwifery.* New York: Howell Book House, 1994.

ABOUT ACTIVITIES

American Rescue Dog Association. *Search and Rescue Dogs.* New York: Howell Book House, 1991.

Barwig, Susan and Stewart Hilliard. *Schutzhund.* New York: Howell Book House, 1991.

Beaman, Arthur S. *Lure Coursing.* New York: Howell Book House, 1994.

Daniels, Julie. *Enjoying Dog Agility—From Backyard to Competition.* New York: Doral Publishing, 1990.

Davis, Kathy Diamond. *Therapy Dogs.* New York: Howell Book House, 1992.

Gallup, Davis Anne. *Running With Man's Best Friend.* Loveland, Colo.: Alpine Publications, 1986.

Habgood, Dawn and Robert. *On the Road Again With Man's Best Friend.* New England, Mid-Atlantic, West Coast and Southeast editions. Selective guides to area bed and breakfasts, inns, hotels and resorts that welcome guests and their dogs. New York: Howell Book House, 1995.

Holland, Vergil S. *Herding Dogs.* New York: Howell Book House, 1994.

LaBelle, Charlene G. *Backpacking With Your Dog.* Loveland, Colo.: Alpine Publications, 1993.

Simmons-Moake, Jane. *Agility Training, The Fun Sport for All Dogs.* New York: Howell Book House, 1991.

Spencer, James B. *Hup! Training Flushing Spaniels the American Way.* New York: Howell Book House, 1992.

Spencer, James B. *Point! Training the All-Seasons Birddog.* New York: Howell Book House, 1995.

Tarrant, Bill. *Training the Hunting Retriever.* New York: Howell Book House, 1991.

Volhard, Jack and Wendy. *The Canine Good Citizen.* New York: Howell Book House, 1994.

General Titles

Haggerty, Captain Arthur J. *How to Get Your Pet Into Show Business.* New York: Howell Book House, 1994.

McLennan, Bardi. *Dogs and Kids, Parenting Tips.* New York: Howell Book House, 1993.

Moran, Patti J. *Pet Sitting for Profit, A Complete Manual for Professional Success.* New York: Howell Book House, 1992.

Scalisi, Danny and Libby Moses. *When Rover Just Won't Do, Over 2,000 Suggestions for Naming Your Dog*. New York: Howell Book House, 1993.

Sife, Wallace, PhD. *The Loss of a Pet*. New York: Howell Book House, 1993.

Wrede, Barbara J. *Civilizing Your Puppy*. Hauppauge, N.Y.: Barron's Educational Series, 1992.

Magazines

The AKC GAZETTE, The Official Journal for the Sport of Purebred Dogs. American Kennel Club, 51 Madison Ave., New York, NY.

Bloodlines Journal. United Kennel Club, 100 E. Kilgore Rd., Kalamazoo, MI.

Dog Fancy. Fancy Publications, 3 Burroughs, Irvine, CA 92718

Dog World. Maclean Hunter Publishing Corp., 29 N. Wacker Dr., Chicago, IL 60606.

Videos

"SIRIUS Puppy Training," by Ian Dunbar, PhD, MRCVS. James & Kenneth Publishers, 2140 Shattuck Ave. #2406, Berkeley, CA 94704. Order from the publisher.

"Training the Companion Dog," from Dr. Dunbar's British TV Series, James & Kenneth Publishers. (See address above).

The American Kennel Club produces videos on every breed of dog, as well as on hunting tests, field trials and other areas of interest to purebred dog owners. For more information, write to AKC/Video Fulfillment, 5580 Centerview Dr., Suite 200, Raleigh, NC 27606.

Resources

Breed Clubs

Every breed recognized by the American Kennel Club has a national (parent) club. National clubs are a great source of information on your breed. You can get the name of the secretary of the club by contacting:

The American Kennel Club
51 Madison Avenue
New York, NY 10010
(212) 696-8200

There are also numerous all-breed, individual breed, obedience, hunting and other special-interest dog clubs across the country. The American Kennel Club can provide you with a geographical list of clubs to find ones in your area. Contact them at the above address.

Registry Organizations

Registry organizations register purebred dogs. The American Kennel Club is the oldest and largest in this country, and currently recognizes over 130 breeds. The United Kennel Club registers some breeds the AKC doesn't (including the American Pit Bull Terrier and the Miniature Fox Terrier) as well as many of the same breeds. The others included here are for your reference; the AKC can provide you with a list of foreign registries.

American Kennel Club
51 Madison Avenue
New York, NY 10010

United Kennel Club (UKC)
100 E. Kilgore Road
Kalamazoo, MI 49001-5598

American Dog Breeders Assn.
P.O. Box 1771
Salt Lake City, UT 84110
(Registers American Pit Bull Terriers)

Canadian Kennel Club
89 Skyway Avenue
Etobicoke, Ontario
Canada M9W 6R4

National Stock Dog Registry
P.O. Box 402
Butler, IN 46721
(Registers working stock dogs)

Orthopedic Foundation for Animals (OFA)
2300 E. Nifong Blvd.
Columbia, MO 65201-3856
(Hip registry)

Activity Clubs

Write to these organizations for information on the
activities they sponsor.

American Kennel Club
51 Madison Avenue
New York, NY 10010
(Conformation Shows, Obedience Trials, Field
Trials and Hunting Tests, Agility, Canine Good

Citizen, Lure Coursing, Herding, Tracking,
Earthdog Tests, Coonhunting.)

United Kennel Club
100 E. Kilgore Road
Kalamazoo, MI 49001-5598
(Conformation Shows, Obedience Trials, Agility,
Hunting for Various Breeds, Terrier Trials and
more.)

North American Flyball Assn.
1342 Jeff St.
Ypsilanti, MI 48198

International Sled Dog Racing Assn.
P.O. Box 446
Norman, ID 83848-0446

North American Working Dog Assn., Inc.
Southeast Kreisgruppe
P.O. Box 833
Brunswick, GA 31521

Trainers

Association of Pet Dog Trainers
P.O. Box 3734
Salinas, CA 93912
(408) 663–9257

American Dog Trainers' Network
161 West 4th St.
New York, NY 10014
(212) 727–7257

**National Association of Dog Obedience
Instructors**
2286 East Steel Rd.
St. Johns, MI 48879

Associations

American Dog Owners Assn.
1654 Columbia Tpk.
Castleton, NY 12033
(Combats anti-dog legislation)

Delta Society
P.O. Box 1080
Renton, WA 98057-1080
(Promotes the human/animal bond through
pet-assisted therapy and other programs)

Dog Writers Assn. of America (DWAA)
Sally Cooper, Secy.
222 Woodchuck Ln.
Harwinton, CT 06791

National Assn. for Search and Rescue (NASAR)
P.O. Box 3709
Fairfax, VA 22038

Therapy Dogs International
6 Hilltop Road
Mendham, NJ 07945